COMMUNICATIONS

FOR

VOLUNTEERS

LOW-COST STRATEGIES FOR COMMUNITY GROUPS

Louise Merrington

First published in 2017 by PAC Books

www.pacbooks.com.au

Cover image by IconicBestiary/iStock
Cover design by Louise Merrington
Author photo by James Walsh
Internal graphics by Louise Merrington
Editing by Maxine McArthur
Formatting by Perry Elisabeth Design

ISBNs:
Mobi format: 978-0-6480215-1-3
Epub format: 978-0-6480215-2-0
Paperback format: 978-0-6480215-0-6

National Library of Australia Cataloguing-in-Publication entry:
    Merrington, Louise, author.
    Communications for volunteers: low-cost strategies for community groups /
    Louise Merrington.

    ISBN 9780648021506 (paperback)
    Includes bibliographical references.
    Community organization--Australia--Communication systems.
    Nonprofit organizations--Australia--Marketing.
    Volunteers--Australia--Handbooks, manuals, etc.

About the Author

Dr Louise Merrington is the director of Pure Arts Communications, a boutique communications consultancy that specialises in providing communications and outreach training and consultancy services to universities, companies, community groups, researchers and practitioners working in the humanities, arts and social sciences.

Louise holds a Bachelor of Arts (Hons) in Media and Communications/Chinese from the University of Melbourne and a PhD in international relations from the Australian National University (ANU), where she wrote her thesis on the China–India political relationship.

Louise has worked as a journalist, strategic analyst, editor, facilitator and university communications manager. She is currently completing a book based on her PhD thesis, tentatively titled *India and China in the Asia-Pacific, 1890-2030*, as well as two more communications handbooks, *Communications for Academics* and *Communications for Artists*. Her first novel, a Gothic mystery called *Greythorne*, was published by Pan Macmillan Australia imprint Momentum Books in 2015, and she is currently finishing her second, *The Iron Line*. Her fiction can be found at http://www.lmmerrington.com.

To be the first to know about newly released books, webinars, courses and other material, please sign up to the Pure Arts Communications email newsletter.

If this book was helpful to you, please leave a review.

Acknowledgements

This book would not have been possible without the help and support of the following people: Simon Brady, Mary-Anne Georgey, Paula Hanasz, Alex Maroya, Mary Lynn Mather, the members of the Freelance Jungle and Clean Indie Reads Facebook groups and, of course, my wonderful husband, Tristan Foon.

Contents

Introduction

This is not a marketing textbook. You won't find any marketing theory in here or any discussions of complex strategies. What you will find are some simple, straightforward, low-cost ways for community groups and other volunteer organisations to maximise their communications, both with their members and the general public.

I've been involved with many community groups over the years, from sports clubs to community bands, theatre groups and choirs, to church councils and social justice organisations. I love volunteering and I'm one of those people who always seems to end up on committees. Since you're reading this, you probably are too. But what I've found is that most community groups tend to lack or only have a basic understanding of communications and marketing strategies. This isn't really surprising, because many of the people who serve on volunteer committees have no background in communications and marketing. However, with the rise of the web and social media, community groups are now operating in a much bigger space, and having at least a basic online and social media presence is now essential. The general public also expects a higher standard of professionalism in communications from community groups than in the past. So what are volunteer committees with limited time and often limited skills to do? Providing some solutions to this problem is why I wrote this book.

There are a few different ways you can use this book. You can read it start to finish, working through developing a communications strategy in Part 1 and then using the specific tools in Part 2 to put it into practice. Or you can dip in and out of the book, just looking at the sections that are most relevant to your organisation.

That said, one of the most common mistakes that I see in my role as a communications consultant—not just from community groups but from companies and other organisations as well—is communication without a defined purpose. Most people and organisations think about their communications method or medium without ever thinking strategically about their audience or message. This means that they feel they have to have a presence everywhere:

on multiple social media networks, on the web and in the traditional media. But because this presence is so wide, it's often spread too thinly and is poorly maintained. Developing a communications strategy will allow you to better target your efforts and save you time and energy. It will ensure that you're only active in the places where you're most likely to reach your audience, rather than trying to be all things to all people. And developing a communications strategy isn't hard: mostly, it's about answering a series of targeted questions, which will give you a better insight into what you want to achieve with your organisation. There's even a series of handy templates at the end of this book that lays out all of these questions for you, and real-life case studies throughout that highlight different aspects of communications, as well as a glossary of specialised terms.

The main emphasis of this book is on things that volunteers in community groups can do themselves with little or no training. Many of the tools discussed here are free or low-cost. However, there will be times when you need to hire professionals, and this book will also give you guidance on how best to spend a limited publicity budget.

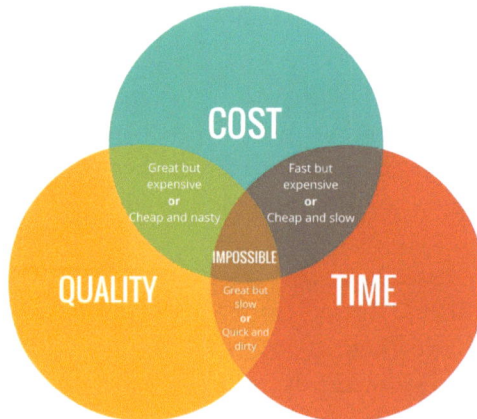

This Venn diagram shows the basics of project management. Its three main variables are quality, cost and time. When you're planning a specific project, you can usually achieve two of these variables, but getting all three—a high-quality product quickly and cheaply—is impossible. What this means for community organisations is that sometimes you'll need to pay for quality or speed. There are many areas where community groups can produce their own work, but getting professional services for things like graphic design, photography, copywriting or editing can make all the difference to the quality of the final product. At the back of this book is a flowchart that will help you decide when to hire a professional, as well as a list of communications-related professions and descriptions of what they do. These include designers, copywriters, editors, photographers and social media specialists. This list will help you select the right person for the job should you need to hire a professional.

AFTER READING THIS BOOK YOU'LL BE ABLE TO:

Develop an external communications strategy for your organisation using a series of steps, from audience identification to media selection, content creation and impact measurement

Develop an internal communications strategy for your organisation to ensure you're connecting with your members in the most effective way possible

Develop a social media strategy based on your external communications strategy

Understand the basic principles of copyright and intellectual property

Understand the basic principles of design for physical publicity materials, and be familiar with free online graphic design tools and stock photo, font and music sites

Have a basic understanding of free web hosting services, as well as the principles of good web design, web copywriting and search engine optimisation

Understand how and why to engage with the traditional media— newspapers, radio and television

Understand the advantages and disadvantages of different social media platforms

Know how to develop email lists using free email marketing software, and how best to employ them

Understand the basic principles of writing in Plain English and know how to improve your writing

Be familiar with other useful tools such as online surveys and petition sites, and crowdfunding

Know when and how to employ a professional

So, where do we start? The best place to begin is with a communications strategy.

PART I –

COMMUNICATIONS STRATEGIES

What is a communications strategy and why do you need one?

Once upon a time, community groups were exactly that: they served the people and communities in their immediate vicinity. Nowadays, however, many community groups draw their membership from a much wider base. People are more inclined to seek out specific interest groups based on factors other than just location, and community groups now have to prove to potential members why these people should choose them.

CASE STUDY

FINDING YOUR UNIQUE VALUE PROPOSITION

The area where I live has a vibrant amateur theatre scene: there are around half-a-dozen amateur theatre groups in a region of about 350,000 people. This means that the market is basically saturated, and amateur actors, directors, musicians and production teams can pick and choose which shows they do. For the theatre companies, it means they have to compete not only for audiences, but also for potential cast and crew members. And this means they need to communicate what their strengths are. Are they an amateur company that produces semi-professional shows and therefore seeks and expects excellence? This will appeal to a particular type of person, probably someone who wants to become a professional actor and is looking to get the best experience they can. Or are they a company with a friendly, familial atmosphere that prides itself on giving everyone a go? This will appeal to people who want to get involved in theatre for fun and to meet new people, but aren't necessarily intending to become professional. Marketers call this the Unique Value Proposition (UVP)—telling everyone what you've got to offer or what problem you can solve.

So what does this mean in practice? Well, it means that community organisations really need to have a communications strategy.

I like to think of it like archery. If you were at an archery range, you wouldn't just shoot arrows here, there and everywhere and hope that one of them hits the target. It's time-consuming and uses a lot of resources for not much return (you might fire twenty arrows but only get one hit). Rather, you'd aim very carefully and do your best to ensure that every single arrow hits the target.

It's the same with communications. Many organisations throw out lots of different ideas and feel that they have to have a presence in a lot of different places. This scattergun approach means their communications often don't reach the people they really need to target, and they end up spending a lot of energy and resources for not much return. At worst, this can lead to burnout of your volunteers (because you're asking them to do a lot of essentially useless work), and spending money—which many community groups don't have much of—on disconnected strategies that don't work.

So what does a communications strategy involve?

The good news is it isn't as scary as it sounds. A communications strategy is, in its most basic form, a list of questions that gets you thinking about who your audience is, what message you want to send to them, and how best you can reach them. It doesn't have to be filled with marketing jargon—it's a simple, straightforward analytical tool. The next three chapters will take you through step-by-step processes for developing three different types of communications strategy, using the templates provided in Appendix A: External Communications Strategy, Appendix B: Internal Communications Strategy, and Appendix C: Social Media Strategy, but first we need to look at the different types of communications.

External and internal communications

Most community groups will need to engage in two types of communication. **External communication** is anything intended for an outside audience. For music or theatre groups, it could be the people you want to come and see your productions; for sports groups, it could be your fans; and for social justice groups it could be the people you want to get involved in your cause or to access your services.

The way you reach these people will depend on who they are and what your aim is, and we'll go into this in more detail when we map out a communications plan. But, broadly speaking, there are four major ways you can reach your external audience:

- Online presence (e.g. website, possibly including an email list)

- Traditional media (e.g. radio, television and newspapers)

- Social media (e.g. Facebook, Twitter, Instagram, Snapchat etc.)

- Physical or 'real-world' publicity (e.g. events, posters, fliers)

You don't necessarily have to use all these methods, although a good website these days is really non-negotiable. Both traditional and social media have two aspects: free and paid. In both cases, you can get free exposure through articles or posts, or you can pay for advertising. Chapter 6 looks at how to engage with the traditional media, while Chapter 7 covers social media in a lot more detail, including the advantages and disadvantages of paid advertising. Chapter 4 gives an overview of events and physical publicity materials.

Internal communication is anything intended for your members. For religious organisations, these are parishioners; for music and sports groups they're the people who make up your choir or your sports team. For social justice groups they're the people who run your activities. In almost all community organisations, these are also the people from whom the governing committee or body is drawn.

Many organisations make the mistake of neglecting internal communications, and as a result members often feel like they've been forgotten or that they don't know what's going on in their group. The other mistake organisations make is to think that internal communications is purely one-way: missives from the governing body down to the members. In fact, the best internal communications strategies map out two-way avenues of communication. For leaders of community groups, it's important not just to tell members about what's going on, but also to have channels for listening to their concerns and ideas.

Some effective internal communications channels include:

- Email newsletters (from the governing body to members; email can also be used as a way for members to contact the leadership)

- Regular social events (where members get to know each other and the group's leadership team and relationships are strengthened)

- Surveys (so the leadership can find out what members think; these are easily conducted online)

- Social media (especially closed groups on Facebook)

When thinking about internal communications, it's vital that the leadership team doesn't neglect face-to-face connections. It can be tempting to do it all by email, but there's really no substitute for strong interpersonal relationships and good governance practices. These are vital in any workplace, but particularly for groups that are run by volunteers, because if those people aren't feeling valued and satisfied then they have no other incentive (such as a salary) to stay on, and poor word-of-mouth can lead to serious reputational damage for the organisation.

The other important thing to remember is that, in general, you need to communicate around three times as much as you think you do. This is particularly true if your organisation is going through a difficult time or is working on a major project, such as fundraising.

You've probably noticed that social media is a useful tool for both external and internal communications. For this reason, I'd recommend that, if you've identified social media as a big part of your communications strategy, you draw up a separate social media strategy as well, using the template in Appendix C.

Chapter 1

External Communications Strategy

IN THIS CHAPTER, YOU'LL LEARN HOW TO:

Identify the purpose of your communications

Identify your audience

Identify your message

Identify your best medium

Create engaging content

Measure the impact of your strategy

Audit your communications channels

Many groups—not just community organisations, but businesses as well—make the mistake of ignoring the 'strategic' part of communications and rushing straight into the nuts and bolts of communicating. However, if you don't take the time to plan your communications—essentially asking yourself who you're communicating with and why—you'll end up wasting a lot of time and effort on ineffective strategies. In this chapter, you'll learn how to develop a simple yet comprehensive external communications plan.

1.1. Developing an external communications strategy

This chapter will take you through the external communications strategy template in Appendix A, explaining the different sections and how to optimise your answers to get the best results.

The most important thing to remember is to be as specific as you can. The more general your answers, the less effective your strategy.

Step 1: Identify your purpose

Why do we want to communicate with people? What are we aiming to achieve?

One of the biggest mistakes organisations make is to rush straight to the end of the communications process—identifying messages and media—without asking why they want to communicate with people in the first place. For most community groups, the answer to this question will be a variation of 'Because we want people to get involved with us,' but it's worth interrogating that statement a bit more to really figure out *why* you're communicating. For example, do you want to entertain people, or give them information about a particular issue or event, or affect policy outcomes, or promote social change?

The basic rule of thumb is that all communication should be either a) entertaining; b) useful; or c) both. You either need to be entertaining people, telling them about something they didn't know before or solving a problem for them.

CASE STUDY

IDENTIFYING YOUR COMMUNICATION PURPOSE

Here are some examples of possible communication purposes from a random selection of community groups.

University club for international students
Purpose: To provide a supportive community for people who are far away from home
Solving a problem: loneliness and isolation

Sports club
Purpose: To get people to play for and support our team
Solving a problem: Giving people a place to play sport
Entertainment: Providing engaging matches

Refugee action group
Purpose: To inform the general public about the plight of refugees
Information: Telling people things they didn't know about refugees, and thereby attempting to affect government policy by encouraging people to take action
Solving a problem: Helping refugees integrate more easily into their new homeland

Community brass band
Purpose: To provide engaging concerts by and for the local community, including at civic events
Entertainment: Providing shows for the local community
Solving a problem: Giving musicians in the local community a place to play

Once you've identified your reasons for communicating, you can move on to look at who you want to be communicating with.

Step 2: Identify your audience(s)

What are the demographics of the people we are trying to reach?

Whom you're trying to reach will have a huge impact on the communication methods you use, and choosing the wrong channel for your audience will mean your message doesn't reach the people you want it to. It's possible—indeed, likely—that you'll have more than one audience, so in this section make sure you give a separate set of answers for each audience you identify. The aim of this question is to build up a broad picture of your ideal customers. Once you understand who they are and what they like to do, you'll be able to figure out how best to reach out to them. Demographics regarding interests, cultural preferences and information consumption are more important than age or gender, unless your organisation is catering specifically to people of a particular age or gender.

- **Age.** This is important if your organisation caters to people in a specific age group, such as children or the elderly.

- **Gender.** This is important if your organisation caters to people of a particular gender, e.g. a men's shed.

- **Location.** Are you targeting people just within your local area, within a wider region, state or province, nationally or internationally?

- **Nationality/ethnicity.** This is important for organisations that are targeting people from specific backgrounds, e.g. university clubs for international students.

- **Language.** Do you need to present your information in multiple languages?

- **Interests/hobbies.** This is one of the most important things to identify, as most community groups tend to be interest-based. What do these people like to do? Once you know that, you can start to figure out where they hang out and how to reach them.

- **Financial status.** This is particularly important if your main goal is fundraising. You'll need to decide if you're seeking to target wealthier people who can give more money, or less-wealthy people who can be active in other ways. It's also important for groups that are putting on shows or events that you're charging people money to attend, because it will affect your pricing.

- **Buying habits**. What does your audience spend their money on? This is related to their interests and also their financial status.

- **Computer literacy**. Do they use computers and the internet? If so, how much? Think also about *how* they access the web (primarily on smartphones and tablets, or on desktops?). Do they use a lot of social media?

- **Information consumption habits**. How do these people like to find out about things? Through the internet and word of mouth on social media? Through local and national newspapers or radio? Or through a different way altogether?

Step 3: Identify your message

What are we trying to say? Why should people care? Why is this newsworthy at this time?

Once you're figured out who your audiences are, you need to think about the point you most want to get across to them. This is very similar to developing an 'elevator pitch' for a book or project—try to summarise your primary message in one sentence. If you have more than one audience, you may find you need to adjust the message slightly or emphasise different things for different audiences.

A secondary question that's particularly important to ask, especially if you're thinking about approaching the traditional media, is 'Why is this newsworthy right now?' We'll discuss the specific details of what makes a topic newsworthy when we look at engaging the traditional media in Chapter 6 but, bluntly speaking, why should anyone care about what you have to say?

Unfortunately, there are two factors working against you here. Firstly, people's attention spans are very short, and secondly, you're competing for their attention in a media environment that is incredibly 'noisy'. If you want to get your audience's attention and retain it, you need to be able to explain to them quickly and succinctly why what you're doing matters to them.

CASE STUDY

DEVELOPING YOUR 'ELEVATOR PITCH'

An 'elevator pitch' is the one-sentence summary that you'd give to someone in an elevator if they asked you about your organisation (it needs to be short enough for you to get through it before they get off at their floor!).

Open to all, with the aim to provide a venue and opportunity for men to meet, socialise, exchange and develop both practical and life skills in a safe and supportive environment.

This is the summary of a local Men's Shed, as found in an online directory of community organisations. In one sentence it sums up:

- Who it's open to

- What its purpose is

- What the people who attend will get from it.

Step 4: Identify your medium(s)

What is the best way to reach our audience(s)?

The media channels that work best for you will depend on your audience and your organisation's focus. If your work is closely tied to the news cycle and/or primarily targets elite figures such as government policymakers or businesspeople (e.g. social justice groups), writing op-eds for newspapers could be an effective way to engage with public debate. However, if your work is more local, or has a more specialised audience (e.g. arts or sports groups) you may find it better to tap into interested communities via social media.

There are two main questions to ask about your audience when thinking about the mediums that will reach them best:

- How do they like to access information?
- Where do they hang out, both physically and online?

If you're targeting an audience that is less likely to access information online, such as older people (speaking in demographic generalisations), then you'll probably get better results through the traditional media and through physical publicity materials like fliers and posters than through social media. Conversely, if your audience is teenagers, then a social media presence is absolutely crucial. Here you can see some of the pros and cons of different media types.

MEDIA TYPES

The pros and cons of using different types of media to promote your organisation

• • • • •

TRADITIONAL NEWS MEDIA

PROS
Respected
Quality-controlled
Widely read
Influential
Sometimes paid

CONS
Heavily dependent on news cycle
Quick turn-around time
Difficult to break into
Distinctive writing style

WEBSITE

PROS
Brand and message control
Can be built easily and cheaply

CONS
Difficult to grow reach
Time-consuming to maintain
Requires familiarity with IT

SOCIAL MEDIA

PROS
Highly visible
Wide reach
Can target niche interests

CONS
Easily trolled
Hard to cut through 'noise'
Needs regular maintenance
Requires original content

Think also about opportunities for cross-promotion; for example, if you're a theatre group with an upcoming production, see if you can advertise in other theatre groups' show programs in return for them advertising in yours. A lot of freelance or independent creative professionals band together for collective promotions, as you reach not only your existing audience but also those of your collaborators.

Step 5: Create your content

What's the most engaging way to get our message across?

Once you've worked out who you're targeting and what medium you plan to use, you need to decide which type of content will work best. An 800-word article might be appropriate for traditional or some online media channels, but photos and videos tend to get greater reach on social media. Think about your audience and what sort of content they're likely to respond best to—some audiences might be fine with reading a full article, but younger people will probably prefer their media to be visual, short and engaging.

As discussed above, regardless of the form, content must be one of two things: useful or entertaining.

A useful tip here is repurpose your content. You don't have to dream up something completely new each time—just think about the ways you can make the same thing work for you multiple times in different channels. This doesn't mean reposting exactly the same thing across all your channels—that risks boring your audience—but rather drawing out different aspects of the one piece. Articles that appear in newspapers or online outlets can also generally be republished—you just need to make sure you get permission from the original publisher. Most newspapers, magazines and websites are fine with this as long as the republished article links back to the original.

This type of repurposing is particularly relevant to social justice organisations or other groups that work in political or otherwise topical areas. If you work on a topic that will hit the news at some point (e.g. asylum seekers) you can have the body of an article written so that all you need to do is 'top-and-tail' it (add an introduction and conclusion) to make it relevant and then submit it to the appropriate outlet. See Chapter 6.3 for more on this.

Photos, graphics and videos work particularly well on websites and social media (especially Instagram, discussed in Chapter 7.3) but they need to be high-quality and used judiciously. Research has shown that 30 seconds is when people start to switch off from videos, and that number is getting shorter as attention spans decline. Ideally, any videos intended for social media should be under two minutes, or under one if possible. This doesn't sound like long, but I can tell you from experience that, looking at the metrics of videos I've posted on

YouTube or Facebook, I notice big drop-offs in the number of viewers at 15 seconds and often again at 30. The lesson here is to get all your most important information up front. Also bear in mind the differences in platforms. YouTube videos automatically play with sound, but videos on Facebook play without sound until the user clicks on it. Therefore, videos intended for Facebook work better if they have engaging text at the start. For most volunteer organisations, video probably won't be the medium of choice. However, it's worth thinking about, especially if your organisation produces highly visual work (e.g. arts organisations, or those that use archives extensively, like genealogy or historical societies). We discuss video production more in Chapter 4.6.

Ultimately, the only thing limiting your content is your creativity, time and skills. There are new tools becoming available every day that mean it's never been easier to create low-cost, high-quality content, and we're going to explore many of these in later chapters. The main thing to remember is *your content must always serve your audience, and it must always be either entertaining, useful, or both.*

Step 6: Measure your impact

How many people are we engaging with effectively?

The principle here is 'chase leads, not likes.' Your aim is to get people to actively engage with your organisation. Particularly on social media, this means encouraging people to engage in discussion rather than just 'liking' a post. Basic statistics—such as numbers of followers or likes—are secondary to other measurements such as sentiment, reach/impressions or growth (in layman's terms: How do people feel about your brand? How many people are seeing your products or messages? Are you reaching more people over time?). You're much better off having a small group of highly engaged followers than thousands who don't engage. This also means that you can't just be a passive user—you need to start the conversation and engage with other people's content and respond to comments as well. We'll discuss this more when we look at planning a social media strategy in Chapter 3.

There are many tools available to measure online reach. Facebook and Twitter have inbuilt measurement tools, and Google Analytics can provide detailed feedback on website traffic (if you build a website using WordPress or similar sites there are also inbuilt analytics tools included). Creating short links for use on Twitter and Facebook can also allow you to see how many people have clicked through your link and where they've come from. These metrics can be useful, in that they will give you information on things like demographics and the time of day your followers are online, which can help you decide what and when to post. Chapter 5, which looks at developing your website, discusses this in more detail.

The aim of this isn't to turn you into marketers—it's to give you some data so that you can make informed decisions about what's working and what's not. Much like a business plan, a communications plan shouldn't be static: You should aim to revise it at least every 12 months. If the metrics show that you're not getting the results you desire, take action to fix this, such as changing the type of content you're producing or the outlets you're producing it for.

Step 7: Audit your channels

Are there channels we haven't been using that we should be? Are the channels we're currently using giving us good results?

Once a year, take stock of your communications strategy and decide if the platforms you're using are working for you, or if you perhaps need to build up new channels or close existing ones. This is especially relevant to social media.

OVERVIEW

Understand why you're communicating. What do you want to achieve?

Identify your organisation's Unique Value Proposition. What makes it different from other similar groups?

Know your audience—who they are, what they like, and how you can best reach them.

Develop an engaging message and appealing content. Why should people care about what you have to say?

Choose the communication medium that your audience is most likely to use.

Monitor your results and change your tactics if necessary.

Chapter 2

Internal Communications Strategy

IN THIS CHAPTER, YOU'LL LEARN HOW TO:

Identify your organisation's strategic direction

Identify your communication purpose

Conduct an internal communications audit

Identify your audience, messages and mediums

Create engaging content

Measure the impact of your strategy

Develop feedback channels and foster community spirit

2.1. Developing an internal communications strategy

Internal communications is an area that is often neglected by organisations. At its highest level, an internal communications strategy should outline where you currently are as an organisation, where you aim to be, how you plan to get there and how you'll measure whether you've achieved your goals. The 'communications' part is about how you communicate this strategic vision to your members, but if you don't have a vision or plan in the first place then no amount of communication will help, as your members will be able to see through any attempts to paper over the organisation's issues.

The thing to remember is that, even if your organisation doesn't have a specific communications plan, communication is still taking place—it just may not be the kind you want or need. In the absence of official messages from the leadership, especially if the organisation is going through a difficult period, the rumour mill will fill the vacuum. This is both unhelpful and difficult to recover from, as it represents a breakdown of trust between the leadership and members.

To avoid this happening, it's useful to have an internal communications plan. Note that *internal communications is **not** public relations*. Do not try to 'spin' your message or in any way obfuscate. Internal communications is all about clarity of strategic direction and information, and providing your members with the things they need to know in order to help achieve your organisation's aims. *It is also two-way.* Your internal communications plan should not only detail how you communicate with your members, but also how they can communicate with you and what you'll do with the information they provide you (hint: don't just shove it in a drawer—act on it, or you risk losing trust and damaging morale). This template will help you develop a basic internal communications strategy. There are many online resources available for developing more complex internal communications strategies, but these are usually aimed at larger companies, and this template should be adequate for most community groups.

Step 1: Identify your organisation's strategic direction

- Where are we currently at?

- Where do we want to be (organisational goals/objectives)?

- How will we achieve these objectives (step-by-step plan)?

- How long will it take?

- How will we know when we've achieved them (measurement)?

This step will probably take you as long to complete as all the other steps combined, but it's the most important, and the more detail you can go into, the better. Your leadership team needs to have a clear idea of where your organisation is heading and how you're planning to get there so that this can be clearly communicated to members. If the strategic direction is unclear, members may not understand why they need to do certain things, and may feel like they're not being heard. This can erode trust with the leadership team and negatively affect morale. Because volunteers have no financial incentive to stay, members who become disenchanted may leave, which will have flow-on effects for the group's morale, skill base and possibly financial status.

CASE STUDY

IDENTIFYING YOUR MISSION STATEMENT

When you're identifying your organisation's strategic direction and organisational goals, you may choose to write these as a mission statement. It's important that this is specific, unambiguous and doesn't use terms that can be interpreted in several ways.

A local arts organisation identifies its mission as *Providing a nurturing and supportive creative community for artists.* The committee developing the statement intends 'artists' to be interpreted extremely broadly—visual and performing artists, writers, musicians and others, both professional and amateur. However, the person responsible for publicity reads this statement and, being a painter herself, interprets 'artists' to mean only visual artists. She therefore targets all the organisation's external communications to only visual artists, thereby excluding a large number of people that the organisation actually wants to reach.

Step 2: Identify your purpose

Why do we need to communicate? What are we trying to achieve by this communication? How will this help us meet the organisational goals identified in Step 1?

Once you've developed a strategic direction and some organisational goals, you need to work out which parts you need to communicate to your members—why do you want to communicate certain things? Bear in mind that more communication is better than less, because your members need a sense of purpose to understand where the organisation is going and what their role in it is.

Step 3: Conduct an audit

What methods are we currently using to communicate with our members? How do our members currently communicate with the leadership team? How do our members stay in touch with each other?

You're probably already engaged in some sort of communication with your members, whether that's through email, a print newsletter, social media or face-to-face meetings (or a combination of these). Before you can work out how to streamline this, you need to have a clear understanding of what you're currently doing. Think broadly and don't forget that face-to-face communication is just as important as email, if not more so.

If you don't already have a good idea of how your members like to communicate—with each other and with the leadership team—then you'll need to do some sort of survey or data-gathering exercise at this stage. This survey could also include questions about the type of information members most want to receive from the leadership team. See Chapter 10.1 for details of SurveyMonkey, a tool that can help with this.

Step 4: Identify your audience(s)

Who do we need to communicate with?

Depending on the complexity of your organisation, you may have several different internal audiences. Two of these will probably be your general membership and your leadership team. So don't just think about communications from the leadership team to the members—think also about communications from members to leaders, and also the leadership team's communications to itself. How does it organise its meetings, documents and strategies? Are there ways these can be streamlined?

Step 5: Identify your message(s)

What do we want/need to say to our members?

As in the external communications strategy, you will need to identify discrete messages for each of your audiences. For example, these could be regular updates on the organisation's strategic direction or finances, or a weekly newsletter of events.

Step 6: Identify your medium(s)

How can we best reach our members? How do they prefer to receive information?

As part of your audit in Step 3, you should have identified how your members would like to receive information. Now that you have this information, you can easily see if your current communications are being delivered in the way your members prefer. If not, you need to change the mediums you're using. Remember to include face-to-face communications in this.

Step 7: Create your content

What's the most engaging way to get our message across?

As detailed in the external communications strategy section, your content needs to be either useful or entertaining, or preferably both. Make sure your messages are organised so that you have adequate version control and don't send out the same thing multiple times (unless you're doing so for a specific reason). If you have an event coming up that you need to communicate with members about, draw up an event-specific content calendar, noting what you'll be sending out in the weeks before the event and what purpose these communications will serve (what actions do you want your members to take as a result?).

In general, it's worth taking the time to draw up a content calendar or plan for at least the next three months so that your whole leadership team knows what communications will be going out to members and why. This can be as simple as a table with dates noted, or adding notes to a shared calendar.

Step 8: Measure your impact

How many of our members are we engaging with effectively?

Tools like MailChimp (Chapter 8) are essential for managing email lists. Not only do they provide professional-looking templates, but they also give you access to a wide range of analytics such as open rates and click-throughs. This means you can send an email to your list then keep track of how many people are opening it versus deleting it without reading it. If you're getting low open rates you may need to rethink your use of this medium—are people ignoring your emails because they don't find the content engaging, or do they simply dislike receiving emails? Your website and social media accounts provide access to similar analytics, so make sure someone on your leadership team understands how to use them and monitors them regularly.

Make sure you keep your email lists and social media groups up to date, removing people who have left your organisation and adding new members, to avoid spamming people and ensure you're reaching everyone you need to. If your membership base isn't current, this will also skew your data collection. Assign someone on the leadership team to take care of this monthly if you have a regular turnover of members. Organisations with less turnover could do it quarterly or even annually.

Even if face-to-face communications are your primary method, you should still have some way of keeping track of their effectiveness. For example, how many people regularly attend your meetings? Does this change dramatically over time? If so, what might be an explanation for this? Just keeping a simple spreadsheet with some of these figures can help you to spot any trends and address issues early.

Step 9: Develop feedback channels

How can our members best contact us to share their ideas or concerns? Do our members currently feel that they can communicate easily and efficiently with the leadership team? How will we act on information we receive from them? What processes can we put in place to ensure members' information is acted on appropriately?

Again, as part of the audit in Step 3, you should already have got a good idea of your current communication channels and whether your members feel these are adequate. If necessary, tweak these channels or institute new ones to ensure your members' needs are being met. It's also useful at this point to develop some written processes for addressing members' concerns or ideas. Having a written process for this that everyone (or an allocated person, depending on your organisation) on the leadership team will adhere to is important for ensuring transparency and making sure that members' concerns are addressed quickly.

Step 10: Develop intra-organisation communications

What is the best way for members to communicate with each other? How can we foster a sense of community in our organisation?

As part of your audit in Step 3 you should have found out how your members like to communicate with each other, and how they prefer to interact with their community in the group. Fostering a sense of community is incredibly important for volunteer organisations, as it's this shared sense of purpose and mutual support that will keep your members present and active. Chapter 7.1 discusses how Facebook groups can be used to great effect by community organisations, but you may also want to think about face-to-face social activities as well. Do your members only see each other when they come together for the organisation's activities, or do they socialise outside as well? What sorts of social activities can you undertake to help members get to know each other better?

Community-building takes time and needs to be kept up—you can't just run a one-off social event and expect miracles to happen. Think about assigning someone from your leadership team to take responsibility for these sorts of activities and for managing online community spaces as well.

OVERVIEW

Internal communications is not optional. If it's done poorly, your organisation will suffer.

Your message must be consistent.

Internal and external communications need to be integrated. Don't tell your members one thing only to have them receive contradictory messages through the media or online.

Tone is extremely important. If in doubt, get someone else to read the email before you send it.

Make sure your messages look professional and 'clean'—no typos.

Your messages must be clear about what's in it for your members (the WIIFM—what's in it for me—factor). Why do they need to know this and why should they care?

As you work through this strategy, put clear processes in place and write them all down to retain institutional memory (because leadership teams in volunteer organisations tend to change quite frequently). Imagine you're inducting a new administration person to manage your communications—how will they know everything they need to straight away? Someone who hasn't been privy to the planning should be able to come in and immediately understand:

- why you're communicating
- what you do regularly
- how you do it
- the channels you use
- the preferred tone and style of your communications
- how you deal with communications from members.

Chapter 3

Social Media Strategy

IN THIS CHAPTER, YOU'LL LEARN HOW TO:

Conduct a social media audit

Set communications goals

Identify key messages

Develop a brand voice

Use paid, owned and earned strategies

Develop a content plan and calendar

Allocate social media management roles

Develop a social media policy

Develop a critical response plan

Measure the success of your strategy

Analyse your data and take action

3.1. What is a social media strategy and why do you need one?

Social media can quickly become overwhelming if it's allowed to get out of control. For this reason, many companies now employ social media managers whose sole job is to look after the brand's social media presence. Volunteer organisations, however, have neither the time nor the money to do this, so it's important to keep the social media beast firmly within its box. If you don't, you risk two things happening: You either burn out the person tasked with managing it; or (more commonly) you let your accounts become inactive, which looks unprofessional, and your overall online presence suffers as a result. A social media strategy is essentially a plan that details how you'll incorporate social media into your overall communications strategy in order to achieve your marketing objectives—who you want to reach and why, which platforms you want to use, the type of content you want to post, and how often you want to post it.

Remember—you don't have to have a presence on every network, just the ones that suit your communications purposes. Less is often more!

3.2. Developing a social media strategy

A social media strategy in this context is part of your external communications strategy. Using social media groups to interact with your members is covered in Chapter 2.1. For details of the pros and cons of each of the major social networks, see Chapter 7.

This section will take you through the social media strategy template in Appendix C. But first, here are some basic definitions of terms you're likely to come across when preparing a social media strategy.

- **Analytics:** The tools available for measuring your content's reach, targeted demographics and other metrics. Social networks have their own analytics for your organisational page (on Facebook, for example, they're called Insights) and you can also use Google Analytics to track your website's performance. Other online tools, such as email clients like MailChimp, also provide analytics as part of their service.

- **Click-through rate:** The number of people who follow a link from an advertisement or post to your nominated website.

- **Conversion rate:** The number of people who, as a result of your social media strategy, undertake the action you've been encouraging them to, such as buying a product or signing up to a newsletter. For example, you may have 100 people click through from a Facebook ad to your website, and 25 of those sign up to your newsletter (which was the goal of your ad).

- **Engagement:** When your followers engage with something you've posted by liking, sharing or commenting on it. Different social networks have different ways of engaging, but they all tend to be built around these three main approaches.

- **Follower/fan:** A person who has chosen to follow you on social media so that your posts automatically appear in their news feed.

- **Pay-per-click (PPC):** A form of online advertising where you pay a certain amount for every click the ad generates to your nominated website.

- **Reach:** The number of people who see the things you post on your social media account. This is usually divided into *organic reach* and *paid reach*. Organic reach is the number of people who see your posts without you having to pay to 'boost' or advertise them. Paid reach is the number of people you reach with an advertisement or boosted post.

- **Sentiment:** How people feel about your brand, as evidenced in the tone of the comments they leave on your social media pages. Sentiment is usually more important than the number of comments.

Step 1: Conduct a social media audit

What's working, what's not, and how can we adjust?

A social media log (such as the table below) is a simple way of auditing your current channels. List each account's follower counts, engagement rates and other properties. This will allow you to see which channels are performing well for you, and which may need a change in strategy or perhaps to be closed altogether.

Social network	URL	Follower count	Average weekly activity	Average engagement rate (interactions/reach)
Facebook	facebook.com/sampleaccount	1000	6 posts per week	3%
Twitter	twitter.com/smplacct	600	12 tweets per week	2.5%
Instagram	instagram.com/sampleact	850	1 post per week	3.5%
LinkedIn	linkedin.com/SampleAccount	150	2 posts per month	0%

There are a number of simple ways to determine your average engagement rate using the built-in analytics tools in your social media accounts. However, none of these methods takes sentiment into account—for example, whether the comments were positive or negative—and they weight all types of interactions equally (so likes are deemed the same as shares, when a share is actually a more committed type of interaction). But they can provide you with a baseline and let you track your growth over time. You just need to ensure you're using the same formula for your ongoing calculations so that you're comparing like with like.

Social media analytics can get vastly more complicated and nuanced than this, so feel free to research this further if it's an area that interests you. However, for most volunteer organisations these basic metrics should be sufficient.

Average engagement rate per post. Count the number of interactions (likes, comments and shares) over a given period, divide it by the number of posts over that same period, then multiply by 100 to get the percentage.

Average engagement rate per fan. Count the number of interactions and divide it by the number of posts, then divide again by your number of fans and multiply by 100 to get the percentage. This has become less useful since some social networks—specifically Facebook—started hiding pages' posts from fans in order to push businesses and organisations into a paid model.

Average engagement rate by reach. Divide the total number of interactions by the number of people reached (the number of people who saw your posts) then multiply by 100 to get the percentage. This is probably the most accurate way to measure engagement.

As well as tracking your average engagement rates, also track the conversion rates from your social channels to your website—not just the numbers who go to your website from each site, but what they do when they get there. Even if you're only getting a small percentage from one channel, if the conversion rate is high then it's worth keeping. For example, your website might receive 20 per cent of its visitors from Twitter, but of that 20 per cent, 75 per cent of them undertake the intended action (such as signing up to a newsletter). Conversely, the website might receive another 50 per cent of its traffic from Facebook, but this only has a conversion rate of 3 per cent. Some of this value will depend on the exact numbers, but the point is not to disregard a channel just because the click-through rates are low—look at the conversion rates as well. Enabling Google Analytics for your website will give you access to this data and more. See Chapter 5.6 for how to do this.

As part of your audit, make sure you have a good understanding of your audience. Go through the demographic checklist in the external communications strategy template and check that you really know whom you're trying to reach. Conduct a survey if necessary (see Chapter 10.1 for how to do this using SurveyMonkey), especially about their social media habits. Ask yourself what value your organisation is adding to your audience now through social media, and what value you want to be adding.

Step 2: Set your goals

How do these contribute to our overall business objectives and other goals as outlined in our external communications plan and/or business plan? Are they SMART (specific, measurable, attainable, realistic and time-bound)?

Your social media strategy needs to be guided by goals that contribute to your organisation's overall objectives. Essentially, you need to see your social media plan as part of your overall business plan, rather than as an end in itself.

These goals should be SMART:

Specific: Identify the precise area for improvement

Measurable: How will you measure success or completeness? Will you be able to tell if it's half-complete? (e.g. 250 new sign-ups to your email newsletter over the next three months is measurable. 'Become more engaging on social media' isn't).

Attainable and Realistic: Look at what you've done previously. Are you overreaching with your goal? Is it realistic in relation to your resources?

Time-bound: Over what time period do you aim to achieve your goal? Don't make it open-ended. Your goal should be related to an overall business objective, and setting a timeframe gives you a concrete way of measuring the effectiveness of your strategy in relation to that objective.

CASE STUDY

SETTING YOUR GOALS

A local community choir is looking for more singers and also hopes to boost its concert attendance. The committee decides that to do this they need to be able to communicate more directly with people who are interested in the choir **(overall business objective)**, and the best way to reach their audience is via Facebook. In order to achieve this, they take the following course of action:

- **Social media goal:** Grow the choir's email list
- **Specific goal:** Get 100 new sign-ups from Facebook
- **Timeframe:** The next three months
- **Measurement:** Use Google Analytics to track how many people visit the choir's newsletter sign-up page from Facebook over the timeframe.

Step 3: Identify your key message

What do we want the public to know about our organisation? (One line only).

Your key message will influence how you talk to your audience. It needs to be succinct and easily understood—sum up what you want the public to know about your organisation in one line. For example, for an amateur theatre group: *We are a friendly, inclusive group that stages high-quality musical theatre performances for the local community at an affordable ticket price.* The key messages here reach both potential performers and potential audience members: the performers know that it's a friendly group where they will be included, but that the quality of the productions doesn't suffer as a result; and the audience knows that the productions are both high-quality and affordable.

You don't necessarily have to use this key message word-for-word in your public communications, but it should be the driving force behind everything you post. Each time you post on social media, ask yourself if this post serves your key message. If it doesn't, reconsider posting it. Doing this will stop your account being overrun by cat videos or other irrelevant content (unless cat videos are part of your key message!).

Step 4: Develop your brand voice

How would we like our audience to describe our brand? How can we get these traits into our brand voice?

Once you've decided on your voice, write guidelines for your social media persona and voice, and check regularly to make sure your posts are adhering to these.

You need consistency in your organisation's communications, especially if they're managed by a number of people. Your tone and voice should be consistent across all your platforms. Developing a brand voice will help you achieve this.

First, you need to decide on the tone of your brand voice. Is it friendly, serious, formal, casual? Start by listing adjectives you'd like your audience to use to describe your brand (e.g. quirky, reliable, professional, fun). Incorporate these into the tone of your social media messages—if your audience expects you to be quirky, your posts can be a bit more off-the-wall, but if they expect you to be professional then your language and tone will need to be more formal. The most important thing is to be authentic. Social media users today (especially the younger generations) are incredibly savvy and can spot inauthenticity a mile away, which will affect the trust they place in your brand.

Once you've developed your brand voice, write guidelines for your social media persona and voice outlining the tone and language you want to use and the types of content you want to share or re-post, and check regularly to make sure your posts are adhering to these.

Step 5: Identify your strategies

Are we using a paid, owned or earned strategy (or some combination of the three)? Identify all your strategies individually so you can track their effectiveness separately.

Consider how you'll support your strategies in terms of the time, people and resources you'll need to allocate.

Once you've identified your social media objectives, you need to decide on some strategies to pursue them. There are three main types of strategy: paid, owned and earned. You will probably employ a combination of all three.

Paid: This is a social advertising strategy (such as boosted Facebook posts or promoted tweets). This involves boosting certain posts that were already popular with your audience, hopefully resulting in a boost to your earned strategy in the form of likes and shares, or developing standalone ads.

Owned: This refers to branded properties that you control and can use strategically, such as your website, blog or social channels. A content strategy would be an owned strategy, e.g. producing content for your blog then publicising it on your social channels. Word-of-mouth exposure through your members is also an owned strategy—you can empower your members so that they want to talk about your organisation naturally in their own online channels.

Earned: This is the strategy with the highest credibility, as it refers to brand exposure through public acceptance and a strong emotional connection with your organisation, e.g. word of mouth, exposure by media outlets, or endorsement by influencers. Essentially, an earned strategy is all about relationships, including positively interacting with your audience online or forming relationships with influencers in your industry. However, an earned strategy can be quite time-intensive, as it's about interacting with people, so you'll need to consider the people, time and resources you'll need to support this strategy.

A successful social media strategy will incorporate elements of paid, owned and earned media, but you should separate them out so you can measure them individually and test their effectiveness over time. You may find that one type of strategy works better for your organisation than others, or that limitations such as time and the ability to create content restrict what you're able to do.

Step 6: Develop a content plan and calendar

Think about your target audience, goals, brand voice, distribution channels and tactics. Who are we communicating with and how? What do we want to achieve with our content? How will we effectively distribute it to our audience?

This builds on the preparation you've done as part of your external communications strategy (identifying your audience) and the early steps of your social media strategy. When creating your content, you need to make sure that it's targeted to your audience, that it's distributed through the channels most likely to reach them, that it's in a form that's most likely to appeal to them, that it serves your key message, and that the tone conforms to your brand voice.

Who will create our content? Which channels will we use to distribute it? How often?

Content can be text (e.g. blog posts), visual (e.g. photos, videos) or a combination (e.g. infographics, multimedia stories, photo essays). It can be original (created in-house), crowd-sourced from your members, or curated from reputable sources (e.g. sharing articles). You can repurpose your content across multiple channels—adapt it so it's suitable in different forms. You can also schedule your content in advance, so you can produce a batch of content to be released over the next few hours or days. Some social networks, like Facebook, allow you to do this directly from your page, but for others, like Twitter, you'll need to use an external social media management tool for scheduling.

Type of content	Source (original/shared)	Audience	Channels	Posting date(s)	Person responsible
Blog post	Original	Website visitors	Website, Facebook	25 Feb	Jane

What are our key dates for internal and external events that we plan to promote on social media? How much lead time will we need to prepare for these?

Social media campaigns for major events need to be planned in advance. For this reason, it's a good idea to map out a content calendar for at least the next six months (ideally a year) that notes all the major events around which you want to run social media campaigns. This will ensure you're able to plan effectively and aren't trying to pull something together at the last minute.

When developing your content calendar, think about the following things for each campaign:

- Over what period of time will you be developing your content?

- What are the release dates?

- What is the overall duration of your campaign?

- How are you going to support the campaign in terms of staffing and resources?

- Who will be responsible for developing and posting content, monitoring feeds and answering questions?

- Do you have the resources to complete your campaign on time and on budget?

- What reporting intervals will you use to periodically evaluate your campaign (monthly, quarterly, semi-annually)?

Step 7: Allocate roles and responsibilities for maintaining social media accounts

Who will take on the roles of social media director, social media manager and social media coordinator? (In smaller organisations these may all be the responsibility of one person.)

Each member of your social media team needs to have defined roles and responsibilities. Ideally, only a small number of people should have access to your organisation's social media accounts, to help keep your account secure and your voice consistent, so it's worth doing an audit of who currently has access and whether they really need it. You may want to consider using a social media management tool if you have multiple accounts, which will make it easier for your team to monitor all your accounts simultaneously. These tools are discussed in Chapter 7.7.

There are three key roles in a social media team. In smaller organisations, one person may fulfil all these roles. You could also decide to organise your team by social network—one person is solely responsible for Facebook, one for Twitter etc.—but this may make things more difficult where you're wanting to cross-post content across multiple networks.

- **Social media director:** Responsible for higher-level planning and final approval of the social media budget, campaigns and strategies.

- **Social media manager:** Oversees the day-to-day running of campaigns and will manage the timelines to ensure that campaign elements are released on time.

- **Social media coordinator:** Publishes content, monitors engagement and responds to comments and questions.

In a volunteer organisation, the person who looks after your social media accounts (and it will usually be one person, although you may have a larger team if you're lucky) can't be expected to do it on a full- or even part-time basis. For this reason, it's good to set clear expectations for these roles and allocate regular times for checking accounts, responding to messages etc. It's important to think about this in relation to your content calendar and make sure your resources (i.e. the amount of time spent by the person/people looking after your social media) are realistic for the type of campaign you want to run.

Who will be responsible for creating content? Will there be times of high-volume activity where we need more people active on our accounts? If so, who will these be and how will we train them?

As part of your content plan, you'll need to decide how much original content you want to create, versus how much curated (i.e. shared) content. Curated content is easier and quicker to produce but original content generally performs better. Once you've decided this, you need to allocate someone to do it. Again, be realistic about what a volunteer can achieve, to avoid burning people out.

From your content calendar you should have a good idea of when times of high-volume social media activity (e.g. a product release, performance or major event) are likely to occur. At these times, you may need to have extra people trained who understand your organisation's social media strategy and policy and are able to help out at short notice, or if the usual manager is unwell or leaves the organisation. Identify these people early and make sure they're familiar with everything they need—and have account access—so that they can jump in if required.

Step 8: Develop a social media policy

Although this won't be necessary for all organisations, for some—especially social justice-focused volunteer groups or those with a political agenda, or anywhere reputation is important—it's a good idea to have a social media policy. Your social media policy needs to explicitly outline the appropriate and inappropriate use of social media by members and emphasise protecting your organisation's integrity, reputation and values. It should contain sections on:

- How your members should use social media

- What kind of use is discouraged

- What process they should follow if they're unsure what's appropriate (i.e. who to contact)

- The consequences for social media misuse

Empowering your members to engage with your organisation's social media—for example, encouraging them to like or share content that appeals to them personally—is a great way to build earned media.

Your policy should also include the sort of content you're happy for your members to share, and if or when they can interact with customers or respond to comments about your organisation. Include examples to illustrate what appropriate and inappropriate content looks like. It should also include contact details for the person they can talk to if they have any questions about what's appropriate, and the consequences of failing to abide by the social media guidelines.

Step 9: Develop a critical response plan

A critical response plan details how you'll respond on social media to a negative event that affects your organisation's brand. Many volunteer organisations may feel that a critical response plan is unnecessary, but it can be a useful exercise to undertake in case of potential reputational damage. Better to have it and not need it than the other way around.

Your critical response plan should contain the following:

- **A social listening protocol for negative sentiment about your brand.** This lets you pick up on negative sentiment early and address problems before they snowball. Basically, you're looking for negative comments or negative mentions of your brand. Some social media management tools will let you search social networks for your brand name with a list of keywords, which can help with this. Who will be responsible for monitoring this activity and at what point should it be escalated?

- **A list of designated decision-makers who are authorised to communicate on your organisation's behalf.** What responsibilities do individuals have (e.g. approving messaging, liaising with the media)? What are their contact details (including in an emergency)? If they're unavailable, who will take their place? How will you manage a crisis that drags on for days or weeks?

- **A step-by-step action plan** for specific situations that would affect your business and the action you'd take to address them. Brainstorm the negative situations that could occur and write down the specific actions you'd take to address them.

- **Pre-approved messages** that can be used in each scenario. Consider the tone—are you being appropriately serious, contrite etc.? Is your response timely? You should aim to respond as quickly as possible, but don't pre-empt the facts.

Scenario	Action steps	Pre-approved messages
1.		
2.		
3.		

Step 10: Measure your success

Measure your results against your objectives at regular intervals to determine what works, what doesn't and what you need to adjust.

What are the baselines, targets and benchmarks we will use to report against?

It's important to set these early so you can use them to gauge the effectiveness of your strategies over time. These benchmarks and targets can be set as part of your social media audit and goal-setting in Steps 1 and 2.

What sort of quantitative measures will we use?

Quantitative measurement refers to numerical values and their growth or decline over time. A good way to track posts is to look at base, reach, engagement and conversion.

- **Base:** Potential audience, e.g. your Facebook or Twitter followers

- **Reach:** How many people your post reached

- **Engagement:** How much engagement it got (likes, shares, comments)

- **Conversion:** What the conversion rate was (e.g. clicks to your website, email list sign-ups)

If there is growth in these numbers it indicates your strategy is appealing to your audience. Base and reach numbers can guide the strategies and tactics you choose to use (e.g. certain strategies will be more applicable to small/large audiences). However, engagement and conversion are more important because they indicate the actions people are taking on your content. Even if you don't have a large audience, if you have a large number of shares and comments then your strategy is working. This is sometimes referred to as 'chasing leads, not likes'—it's better to have a small number of highly engaged followers than thousands who never engage with your posts.

What sort of qualitative measures will we use?

Qualitative measurement is a more nuanced approach, best done on a post-by-post basis, as it deals with things like sentiment that can't be measured by just numbers. For example, the number of comments on your post may have increased, but you also need to look at the sentiment of those comments—are they positive, negative, or somewhere in between? Qualitative measurements are about the relational side of social media, which is hard to measure but arguably the most important.

How long are our reporting intervals?

Your reporting intervals need to make sense for your strategy—generally over weeks or months rather than days, as it can take new strategies time to make an impact.

Step 11: Analyse your data and take action

Based on the insights in Step 10, what action do we need to take to optimise our current social media strategies? Do we need to change course altogether?

You can use the data you gathered in Step 10 to either optimise your current strategy or change course altogether. Once you've gathered the data, analyse it and then decide a course of action based on these insights. For example, if one of your goals was to drive traffic from your social networks to your website, you could use Google Analytics to see which networks are providing the greatest number of referrals, and which specific posts these came from. You could then adapt your content to use more of the tactics that were in your most successful posts. Can they be better targeted, or posted at a different time? Likewise, if you've already tried to optimise your strategy for a particular social network but it still isn't achieving your goals, you may want to try a completely new strategy or even decide that you no longer need to maintain a presence on there.

Do we know what sort of content our community likes best?

Make sure you also monitor the response from your community about what content they like. Have a look at your competitors—benchmarking your organisation against them helps put your numbers into perspective—and see if you can borrow successful elements of their strategies. Once you've got a decent data set, make sure you compare current and historical data to account for seasonal trends.

What are our competitors doing? Can we borrow successful elements from their strategies?

In addition, you can conduct a competitive analysis—how does your competition use social media, and what works for them? Are there elements of their strategy you can adapt to your own? Anything you want to avoid?

Remember to review and adjust your overall social media strategy as your organisation grows and its goals and needs change. Ideally review your strategy at least once a year.

OVERVIEW

Audit your existing social media accounts to see which ones are performing well and which need work.

Set goals for your social media that are SMART: Specific, Measurable, Attainable, Realistic and Time-bound.

Choose to engage only with those social media networks that you know your audience uses.

Identify the key messages you want to communicate.

Develop a brand voice that reflects the image you want your audience to have of your organisation.

Identify whether you'll be using a paid, owned or earned strategy or a combination of all three.

Develop a content plan and calendar that includes key dates, the type of content and who will be responsible for producing and posting it.

If necessary, develop a social media policy so that your members know what is and isn't appropriate to post on your organisation's social media pages.

Develop a critical response plan that details how your organisation will respond in the event of a crisis that threatens its reputation, including nominating a spokesperson and a social media manager.

Set baselines, targets and benchmarks that you can use to measure the success of your strategies. Set regular reporting intervals to gather your data.

Analyse your data against your objectives and adjust your strategies accordingly.

PART 2 –

COMMUNICATIONS TOOLS

Chapter 4

Events and Physical Publicity Materials

IN THIS CHAPTER, YOU'LL LEARN HOW TO:

Understand copyright and intellectual property

Develop physical publicity materials

Use free online graphic design tools

Find free stock photos, illustrations, fonts and music

Use photos and videos in your publicity materials

Promote events and use online ticketing

This chapter provides some tools to help with the 'real-world' or physical communications that are necessary for many volunteer organisations. These include events, and the production of publicity materials such as posters, fliers and banners. It also gives a basic introduction to graphic design and provides some free tools to help improve the quality of your design.

4.1. Copyright and intellectual property

When you're producing your own publicity materials (whether text- or graphics-based), it's extremely important to ensure you don't infringe others' intellectual property. This means that you can't just use whatever pictures, photos, music or fonts you find online—you need to make sure that you have a proper license to use them. At some point, someone created that material, and licensing gives them the opportunity to profit from their creation.

Creative Commons

To quote its website, Creative Commons is "a worldwide non-profit organisation that provides copyright owners with free licences allowing them to share, reuse and remix their material, legally." Individual creators can license their work under a Creative Commons license, which makes it legally available to others to share or modify for free. These licenses are subject to certain conditions—imposed at the creator's discretion—such as only being available for non-commercial use. They generally also require you to credit the original creator and note any modifications that have occurred.

There are many sites that offer fonts, music, sound effects, illustrations and photos under Creative Commons licenses, which are detailed in Chapter 4.4. An alternative is to purchase photos or illustrations from stock photo sites, although subscriptions can be quite expensive. In Australia, New Zealand and the Pacific you can obtain a license to use music from APRA AMCOS, and for text and visual arts from the Copyright Agency. There are similar associations in other countries, and these are also good sources of information about copyright specific to your jurisdiction.

Whichever route you choose, make sure your content is appropriately licensed for your planned use (in particular, check that it's licensed for commercial use) and that you adhere to the terms of that license.

4.2. Physical promotional materials

Improvements in printing in recent years mean it's now quite affordable for organisations to produce physical promotional materials such as posters, banners, pamphlets and postcards. However, before you do, it's worth considering the intended function and distribution of your material.

Generally speaking, there are two major types of physical promotional material: time-limited and general.

Time-limited material

Much as it sounds, time-limited or event-specific material relates to a particular event or otherwise goes out of date, and is of no use to the organisation beyond that time period (except for archival purposes).

Because of the limited utility of time-specific material, it's important to judge your print runs carefully. If you order too many posters or pamphlets you may end up stuck with surplus stock if you don't use them all, which is a waste of money.

General material

General promotional material doesn't contain text or graphics that date quickly, and can usually be used over quite a long period. Examples are informational brochures about the organisation—it's best to keep the content of these general and avoid any references or photos that will obviously date them—and any promotional material with the organisation's logo, such as t-shirts, pens or coffee mugs.

Because general material doesn't date quickly, it's possible to order it in bulk and stockpile it, which makes it more affordable. However, bear in mind that if your organisation undergoes a rebranding, anything with the previous logo or name will be redundant.

Utility and audience

When you're deciding what sort of physical promotional material to produce, you need to think first and foremost about its purpose—what do you want it to achieve and what information do you want it to communicate?—and its intended audience. Are you going for overall brand recognition—in which case, getting a lot of general material with your brand out there could be useful—or are you trying to promote something specific?

If you're producing posters or banners, where will you hang them and how far in advance of your event? Will you need permission to place them there? Would postcards, magnets, pens or bookmarks work better, as they're something your audience can pick up and take away with them? If you're thinking about a newspaper ad, think very carefully about your audience. Do they read physical newspapers, or would you be better off with some sort of online promotion instead? Are there any opportunities for cross-promotion with similar organisations in your area?

CASE STUDY

CHOOSING YOUR PROMOTIONAL MATERIALS

In a town of around 45,000 people, there's a writers' group. This group meets once a month and is a place for writers to get together, share their work, get feedback and do writing exercises. The group promotes itself online (through a website and Facebook page), but also by having stalls at local community markets, festivals and events.

At these stalls, the group hands out two types of promotional material. One is individual two-page stories written by members, which are given away in a 'lucky dip' fashion. The second is bookmarks with the group's logo, website and contact details. Both these materials are targeted at readers and writers, and the bookmark in particular is a good choice, as it's smaller than a flier and has an actual purpose beyond just being promotional material. Writers are almost always avid readers, so they're likely to keep a bookmark and may refer to it in future.

When to hire a professional

If you're producing a graphics-heavy document that you want to use across a variety of formats—such as different-sized posters, banners, pamphlets or programs—it's worth investing in a professional graphic designer, unless you have someone on your team who has strong graphic design skills and understands some of the issues around manipulating graphics files for resizing.

In a nutshell, graphics files are usually 'raster' or 'vector'. Raster images are made up of pixels—thousands of little squares that collectively create an image. Photos are raster images. Vector images are made up of 'paths', which each have a 'vector' (a mathematical formula) that tells the path how it's shaped and the colours it's bordered by. Line illustrations such as cartoons are usually vector images.

This matters because raster images don't hold their form as they scale—if you blow them up too much you start to see the individual pixels. You've probably noticed this if you've ever tried to blow up a low-resolution photo. Vector images, however, can be resized with no loss of fidelity. But unfortunately, untrained people dabbling in graphic design often don't understand this and usually produce raster files, which become problematic when you try to resize them. Trying to fix this after the fact is very difficult—it's much easier to design exactly what you need from the start, and a professional will be able to advise you on this. This is especially important if you want a single image to be used both in print and online, as vector images need to be converted to raster for web use.

In addition, your image may need to be manipulated or redesigned to fit different formats: for example, if you have an A4 portrait-orientation poster you want resized as a large landscape banner, you'll probably have to move text and images to make it fit. A professional graphic designer will have the tools and the skills to do this easily and will be able to work much faster than an amateur.

For a handy decision-making flowchart on when to employ a professional, see Afterword: When Should I Hire a Professional?

4.3. Online graphic design tools

It isn't usually possible or necessary for community organisations to hire graphic designers for everything they produce. Although important documents are best handled by a professional, smaller-scale projects like social media banners, some posters, blog posts, presentations and newsletters can be produced by untrained people using some of the great new tools now available online. Most of these are free for the basic package.

Canva

Canva is an online graphic-design tool that uses templates and a drag-and-drop interface to allow people with no graphic design training to produce professional-looking graphics. It's free if you use your own images or any of Canva's free images, fonts and other design elements, or you can purchase upgraded elements for US$1 each and pay for your design when you download it. Designs can be downloaded as PNG, JPG or PDF files.

Templates include banners and posts for a variety of social networks (Facebook, Twitter, Instagram, Tumblr, Pinterest), infographics, posters, brochures, letterhead, book covers and many more. The templates are particularly useful for social media as they already fit the various social networks' specified dimensions, so you won't have to spend time resizing them.

Canva is integrated with stock photos, photo filters, icons and shapes, and fonts. It is one of a growing number of fully integrated online design tools, and is one of the most popular due to its user-friendly interface. It also recently launched an app so you can design on the go.

Adobe Spark

Adobe Spark is the latest edition to the Adobe Creative Cloud stable, and is a free online tool that aims to compete with Canva. It's broken into three sections: Spark Post, Spark Page (formerly Adobe Slate) and Spark Video. Spark Post creates social media graphics; Spark Page produces photo essays for the web; and Spark Video produces animated videos using graphics and photos.

A major difference between Adobe Spark and Canva is where the final files are stored. Canva lets the user download a high-quality copy of their design, which they can then use however they want. In contrast, Adobe Spark designs are all stored on Adobe's servers—they can be shared on websites or social media, but the viewer is always redirected to an Adobe site.

Adobe Spark is also designed for use on iPhones and iPads (it's not yet available for Android devices). Spark Post, Spark Page and Spark Video each have their own apps.

Adobe Photoshop Sketch

Adobe Photoshop Sketch is an iOS app that lets you create drawings directly onto your phone or tablet and then export them to Photoshop or Illustrator. Designed for artists, it gives more freedom than tools like Canva or Spark. It also supports styluses and other drawing hardware.

GIMP

The Gnu Image Manipulation Program (GIMP) is free, open-source, high-end image editing software. It is a free alternative to expensive image editing software like Adobe Photoshop and can be used for photo retouching, image authoring and image composition. However, its complexity is on par with Photoshop and similar software, so it probably isn't the best choice for someone with no graphic design experience, or who isn't prepared to put in the time to learn some of the nuances.

Prezi

Prezi is online presentation software that integrates motion, animation and graphics, and is part of a growing number of visual storytelling tools. Rather than designing a presentation around a series of slides, like Microsoft PowerPoint, Prezi uses a limitless zoomable canvas to allow the user to develop flowcharts and other graphics and show the relationships between various kinds of data. It has been praised for overhauling the concept of the presentation and as a cure for 'death by PowerPoint', but some viewers may find the motion-heavy style nauseating.

It is available as a 14-day free trial, after which the user must sign up to a plan.

4.4. Stock photo, illustration, font, music and sound effects sites

There are many websites where you can find free stock photos, illustrations, fonts, music and sound effects. However, the caveat to this is you get what you pay for. Although some sites provide high-quality media, others—particularly free stock photo sites—are of considerably lower quality than media that you pay for, both in terms of composition and resolution. However, many paid stock media sites now offer deals where you can purchase media individually rather than needing a subscription.

Most free stock media is licensed under Creative Commons, so you'll need to make sure you adhere to the terms of the license when you use it. If you're getting historical content from libraries, also make sure that you're free to use it.

Some of the most popular free (and paid) stock media sites are detailed below, along with databases for historical images. However, there are literally hundreds of sites out there, so it's worth conducting your own search as well.

Free sites

Flickr

Flickr is a photo-sharing site where users can upload their own photos. It also has a section called The Commons, which collates photos from public archives around the world and is a great source of historical photos. Flickr users can choose different kinds of licenses when they upload their photos. When you conduct a keyword search on Flickr, in the top left corner there is a drop-down box where you can select to display only photos with a particular license (e.g. commercial use allowed). When you click on a particular photo you'll also be able to see the terms of the license and can check if it suits your purposes.

Image Finder

Image Finder was originally started as a search engine for Creative Commons images on Flickr, but it has now expanded to search and display Creative Commons images from various stock photo sites. Unlike other stock photo sites, where you download the images directly, Image Finder sends you to the author's own site to download high-resolution versions.

Foter

Like Image Finder, Foter is a search engine of Creative Commons images, but it is also a public domain database where users can upload their own images. The interface is clean and user-friendly, and the license attributes of each image are easy to find.

Pixabay

Pixabay is one of the most popular free stock media sites due to its large size and accessibility. All its media is licensed under Creative Commons and can be used for any purpose, including commercial use, without attribution. As well as photos, it contains illustrations, vector graphics and videos.

Free Music Archive

The Free Music Archive is a database of public domain and Creative Commons-licenced music, curated by genre. It also contains a handy FAQ section that details the various licenses for its content.

FreeSFX.com

FreeSFX.com is a collection of free sound effects for use in videos or other projects. The sound effects are free for all uses, including commercial use, as long as they're integrated into projects (i.e. they can't be on-sold by themselves).

Public domain archives and databases

Trove

Trove is the National Library of Australia's digitised content platform. It brings together Australian-related content from archives, libraries and research and cultural institutions across the country, including photos, objects, newspapers, maps, music, sound and video, government papers, diaries and letters, and archived websites. It's a great source of historical photos of Australia.

Library of Congress

The Library of Congress in the US has a fantastic online collection of historical photographs and other documents, including newspapers, maps, films and sound recordings.

Smithsonian Institution

The Smithsonian Institution has around 3000 images under public domain usage on its Flickr page.

British Library

The British Library has an extensive digital collection, although it's not as user-friendly as Trove or the Library of Congress sites. However, many of its images are available on the British Library Flickr page and are in the public domain in most countries.

Paid sites

iStock

iStock is a paid stock photo site run by Getty Images, which is a major player in news photography. It contains photos, illustrations, vector graphics, video and audio. You can buy content through either a monthly subscription or through 'credits', which give you a certain number of images. However, it's quite expensive.

Shutterstock

Shutterstock is a paid stock photo site similar to iStock in quality and pricing. It contains photos, illustrations, vector graphics, video footage and sound recordings.

4.5. Photography

Like graphic design, photography is one of those areas where, unless you have someone in your organisation with high-level skills, you really should consider employing a professional. While amateur photos are fine for distribution within your organisation—for example, photos from a major event that you intend to circulate to members—anything that you intend to use for publicity or branding purposes needs to be high-quality. This is particularly true for the web, as websites have become increasingly reliant on multimedia since the introduction of the HTML5 standard, which supports elements such as full-width scrolling photos. A poor-quality photo on a visual-intensive website will drag down the overall quality of your brand. Similarly, in physical publications such as programs or brochures, photos need to be high-resolution (to avoid pixelation) and colour-graded for printing. If you don't know how to do this, it's best to talk to a professional. See the flowchart in Afterword: When Should I Hire a Professional? for further guidance on this.

There are several things you'll need in order to be able to take passable photos:

- A creative eye

- A good camera

- Photo editing software and the ability to use it.

A creative eye

In some ways, having an 'eye' for photos is even more important than your type of camera. A photographer with a good artistic eye can take stunning photos on a smartphone, while a newbie with a high-end DSLR will probably take poor photos (not least because of the complexity of the settings on high-end cameras). One of the best ways to develop your eye is simply to practise, or you can take a formal course. Technical and community colleges, as well as private providers or freelancers, often offer a range of photography courses held in the evenings or on weekends. These range from learning the basics of a DSLR to specialised techniques such as night photography, to how to take high-quality photos on a smartphone. You'll be able to pick a lot up simply by trying things out yourself and looking at online resources, but it can really help to have someone take you through the basics in person.

A good camera

There's a saying that the best camera is the one you have with you, which is why smartphone photos are so popular—most people don't carry a DSLR with them every day, but they'll usually have their phone. What constitutes a 'good' camera for your situation will depend on the types of photos you want to take and the conditions you'll be taking them in. Studio photography, for instance, requires extensive lighting equipment as well as a camera and its associated accessories, while the lenses you'll need for nature or portrait photography differ significantly. It's best to discuss your needs with a professional before you purchase your camera to ensure you're getting something that will meet them. If your organisation will be taking lots of different kinds of photos, go for a good all-round camera.

Many professionals sneer at smartphone photos, and it's true that there are limitations—pixel count and control being two of the major ones. However, learning to take photos with a smartphone will in many ways make you a better photographer. Because you can't rely as much on the camera to compensate or correct things for you, you really have to think hard about fundamental techniques such as composition and lighting. Smartphone photos are also easily shared on social media networks like Instagram, so if Instagram is part of your organisation's social media strategy, then smartphone photography could be the way to go. There are also lots of accessories, such as lenses and tripods, available for smartphones. Photography Concentrate has an excellent guide to smartphone photography, covering both techniques and hardware.

Photo-editing software

Although you should be aiming to get the best possible photo 'in the camera' (i.e. using composition, lighting and other techniques to achieve the best possible shot), your photos will probably still need some post-processing. If you're taking photos on your smartphone, it's possible to edit them directly on your phone, although the functionality is limited. If you're shooting with a DSLR, you can edit your photos on a computer using photo-editing software, of which the Adobe Creative Cloud programs—specifically Photoshop and

Lightroom—are the gold standard. Photoshop Elements (and Premiere Elements for video editing) is Adobe's cheaper, less-powerful editing software, which is designed more for the amateur user. Note that you will need to shoot your photos in RAW format rather than JPEG if you want to edit them later.

Photography is extremely rewarding, and good photos can make all the difference between your brand appearing amateurish and looking really professional. A professional-looking brand will in turn inspire confidence in your audience and members. See the Further Reading section for more in-depth photography resources.

4.6. Videos

Video is a particularly powerful promotional medium if done well, especially on social media. However, there are a few considerations when developing promotional videos for social media.

- They need to be very short (ideally under 30 seconds). Social media analytics show that views drop off dramatically after 15 seconds. Videos on Twitter are limited to 2 minutes 20 seconds, whereas Facebook can host videos of up to 45 minutes. Instagram has specific parameters—for example, the video needs to be square rather than widescreen. There are also restrictions on file sizes, so check the specs of the platform you're intending to post on.

- Because of viewers' short attention spans, the most important information needs to occur at the start of the video, rather than at the end as in a traditional structure.

- Ideally, videos intended for social media should have subtitles. On many social networks, especially Facebook, videos autoplay without sound and the sound only plays if the viewer clicks on the video. Subtitles are also necessary to improve accessibility.

- Videos intended for YouTube don't necessarily need to conform to the above specifications, but in general shorter videos (i.e. under 5 minutes) get more views than longer ones.

There are two major components to video production: shooting the footage, and editing it. This section will discuss some options for shooting video, before looking at two different types of editing software—free or low-cost linear editing software, and professional-grade non-linear editing programs.

Cameras

Digital SLRs

Most DSLR cameras have a video capability, although the options and quality will depend on the type of camera. Some newer DSLRs are able to shoot full high-definition video, or even 4K (ultra high-definition). If you're producing videos for the web, however, you need to keep the file size relatively small, so you may not need these capabilities.

GoPro

GoPro is a popular brand of small, durable, versatile cameras that come with a range of accessories to attach them to helmets, handlebars and other outdoor gear. There are now other similar cameras manufactured by other companies as well. They are all designed to be hardy and were originally marketed to outdoor adventurers. However, they've become increasingly popular in the wider market due to their high-quality images, relatively low price, and convenience and durability.

A GoPro or similar camera won't give you the video functionality of a DSLR, but it is much more portable, more durable, easier to use and produces very high-quality footage, especially outdoors. The footage can then be uploaded to a computer and edited with standard software. GoPro cameras also take still photos, although they tend to be better at video. Because they can be mounted to various things, they can be used in quite innovative ways, such as being mounted to drones for shooting aerial footage.

Smartphones

Cameras on the most recent smartphones have improved to the extent that there are now festivals for films shot entirely on phones. If you're serious about shooting high-quality video on your smartphone, you can also invest in a range of enhancements—both gear and apps—that will turn your phone into a powerful video camera. Accessories include cases, tripods, sliders, stabilisers, lenses, microphones, lights and remote controls. Apps such as Filmic Pro (discussed further in Chapter 10.2) give your smartphone full high-definition capability.

Video editing software

Linear editing is an older-style method based on pre-digital techniques for editing film and audio tape. It requires viewing or listening to the material in sequence then cutting and rearranging it in order. Most digital video editing software is now non-linear and non-destructive, meaning it doesn't alter the original source material. This gives the editor a lot more flexibility.

For professional-grade video editing software to function properly you will need to make sure your computer has enough RAM, a relatively fast processor and a big enough graphics card to support it. See the software manufacturers' websites for exact specifications.

iMovie and Windows MovieMaker

iMovie is Apple software that comes free with Apple desktops and laptops, and also works on iOS devices. Windows Movie Maker is a similar program produced by Microsoft for PCs, which also comes free as part of the Windows software package.

Both these tools provide generally good basic functionality and should be adequate for editing videos for social media or the web. However, if you are planning to do more-complex video production it may be worth investing in professional-grade software.

Final Cut Pro X and Adobe Premiere Pro

Final Cut Pro X and Adobe Premiere Pro are the industry standard non-linear video editing packages. Final Cut Pro X is for

Mac, while Adobe Premiere Pro is for PC. Both have similar functionality, although their interfaces differ slightly and most video editors prefer one or the other. Premiere Pro is part of Adobe Creative Cloud (which also includes programs like Photoshop and Illustrator) so it's interoperable with other Creative Cloud programs, file storage and apps. Both have extensive online tutorials, forums and support. These software packages are relatively expensive and require a computer powerful enough to run them, but if you're doing a lot of video production it's worth investing in a professional editing program. Adobe also produces a cheaper, less-powerful version, Premiere Elements, which is suitable for amateur users.

4.7. Events

Online ticketing sites have made it particularly easy for community groups to host professional-looking events, especially if the venue they're hiring doesn't have its own ticketing system or box office. As well as keeping track of registrations and selling tickets, many of these sites will also let you email registered attendees to update them on any changes to the event.

Eventbrite is probably the best-known online ticketing site, although there are others such as Trybooking, Ticketebo and EventSmart. Eventbrite has country-specific sites for the US, the UK and Australia, while the other ticketing sites are more generic. They all work in similar ways—generally they'll host free events at no charge, and take a commission on paid events. The exact commission rates and terms vary between sites, so it's best to do your research and choose the provider that best meets your needs.

Event promotion

Depending on your event, it may be worth employing some specific promotional strategies to encourage attendance. This is particularly the case if you're running an ongoing event, such as a series of concerts or lectures. These could include giving complementary tickets to reviewers or members of the media in exchange for coverage, or running special offers such as two-for-one deals at times when you know attendance is likely to be lower. Although some community groups are reluctant to do this, feeling that they're giving away things they should be charging for, it's important to think about the longer term, especially if your organisation is built primarily around events. Offering complementary or reduced-price tickets is what economists and marketers call a 'loss leader'—a reduced or free product that aims to hook your customers and drive traffic to other aspects of your brand. The idea is to introduce people to your organisation by getting them to an event that they might otherwise not have attended, which will hopefully then encourage them to attend future events. You can also have facilities set up at the event where people can sign up to your email list—see Chapter 8.2 for more on this.

If you're running a multiple-day event, you may not know at the start which days are likely to be in less demand. It's therefore important to remain agile, monitor your registrations, and have some strategies in place for quickly offering promotions if you need to. These are best developed as part of your overall event planning process, especially if you want to use special material, such as an online promotional offer poster that you can circulate on social media, which would be difficult to design at the last minute. If you have these strategies in place, it's a matter of just activating them as you need them.

OVERVIEW

Always check the licenses on any photos, illustrations, fonts, music or other media that you intend to use, to ensure you're not infringing copyright.

When producing physical promotional materials, consider their intended purpose, distribution and audience, and whether the material is time-limited or general.

If you're producing a graphics-heavy document that you want to use across a variety of formats, it's worth investing in a professional graphic designer.

Free online graphic design tools are great for smaller projects; however, for complex projects or anything involving branding you should consider hiring a professional.

Free stock photo, font, music and illustration sites are great sources of multimedia—just make sure you abide by the terms of any licenses.

High-quality photos will enhance your brand, and poor-quality photos will detract from it; if your organisation doesn't have a good photographer, consider training someone or hiring a professional.

Videos are becoming increasingly prominent on websites and social media. If you use them, make sure they're short, well-structured and have subtitles.

Online ticketing sites will enable you to easily keep track of registrations for your events. Also consider ways you can promote your event through 'loss-leading' special deals or partnerships with similar organisations.

Chapter 5

Websites

These days, having a website is standard for most businesses, volunteer organisations and even many individuals. If someone hears about your group, chances are the web is the first place they'll go for more information, so having a professional-looking, up-to-date, user-friendly website is a must. The good news is that, thanks to the proliferation of template-based software, you no longer need to know how to code to build a functional, eye-catching website. This chapter will mainly focus on using template-based software to build your own site without complex coding.

5.1. Designing your own website

You have a few different options when it comes to building a website for your organisation.

- Code it yourself from scratch. If you're capable of doing this you probably don't need to read any further in this chapter.

- Work with a professional web designer to build a bespoke site. This will get your organisation something unique, but it's an expensive option and you may not be able to maintain it easily yourself.

- Self-host your website using a template-based content management system like WordPress (the difference between WordPress.com and WordPress.org is explained below). This will give you structure so you don't have to code the whole thing from scratch, but you'll still need some familiarity with HTML and will need to be comfortable organising your own hosting and domain name.

- Use a platform such as WordPress.com, Wix, Weebly or Squarespace, which will provide you with drag-and-drop templates that you can use without coding experience, as well as server space and, if you choose, custom domain name registration. This is the most affordable and easiest method for volunteer organisations and people who aren't familiar with coding and web design, but you don't have as much flexibility with these types of sites as you do when you control it all yourself.

You need a really clear idea of the kind of design you want before you start building it. This is particularly important if you're working with a web designer or coding it yourself. Template-based programs such as WordPress, Wix or Squarespace are probably your best choice if you're unfamiliar with web design principles. However, even if you're using a template, there are some things you need to consider about how you want your user to interact with your site (this will affect the kind of template you choose).

There are six main elements of a website that a user will see, all of which will affect their experience:

- **User and business needs.** The most important thing is to identify who your users are and what they want to get out of the website. Both the users and the business need to be aware of what the website does and what they want to get out of it.

- **Information architecture.** This is the structure of your website, also known as navigation. These are the menus and internal links that a user will use to find things on your site.

- **Interaction design.** This is where things are located on a page. It's one step up from looking at the information architecture, because this also starts to take into account placement of content like videos or paragraphs of text. If your website is too cluttered your users will have a poor experience, but there still needs to be enough information for them to quickly find what they need.

- **Visual design.** This is your site's use of colour, styles, typography etc. Your site's visual design gives it aesthetic appeal and personality. In some template-based programs you may have limited control over colours and fonts, especially if you're on a free plan.

- **Brand.** This communicates the personality of the website and your organisation more broadly. You should have consistent brand guidelines across all your physical and online publicity materials, including choice of colours and fonts. A graphic designer can help you with this, and maintaining a visual style guide will ensure it remains consistent.

- **Content.** This is how the website actually communicates with your users. Content can include text, images, video and audio recordings, as well as other kinds of multimedia. See Chapter 5.3 and Chapter 9.2 for more detail about creating content.

Your website must also be responsive and accessible. *Responsive* means your site will adapt itself when it's viewed on devices such as smartphones or tablets. This may change some aspects of the layout, including the menus. *Accessible* means your site should employ techniques to cater for users with visual, auditory, motor or other impairments. For more detail on how to make your site accessible, see Chapter 5.3.

CASE STUDY

THE IMPORTANCE OF RESPONSIVE DESIGN

Below are some smartphone screenshots from the websites of two local historical societies. The first is non-responsive; the second is responsive.

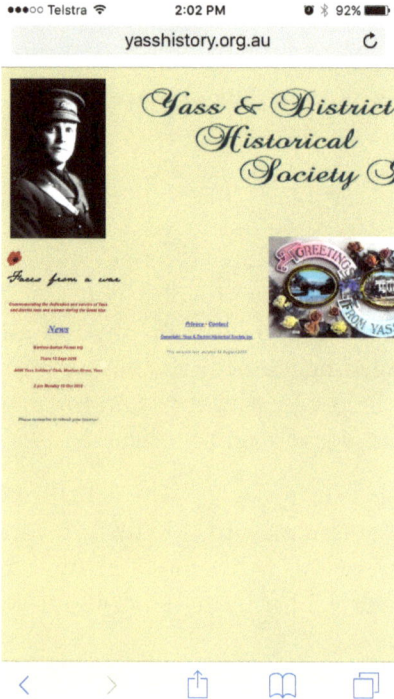

As you can see, the website's heading is off the edge of the phone screen (because it hasn't automatically resized) and the text is very small. The image is also breaking off the edge of the page and the layout in general is difficult to negotiate. Incidentally, zooming in on this site did not fix these problems. Even turning the phone sideways (to give greater width) didn't really help.

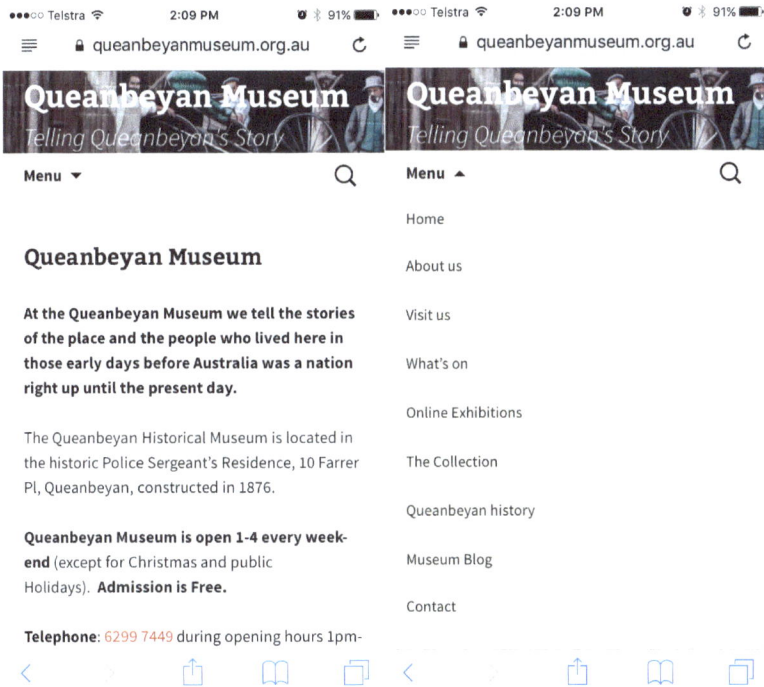

As you can see from these shots, this website fits cleanly into the smartphone screen. Its main heading is clearly visible and the text is big enough to read easily. When you touch the drop-down arrow on the menu bar (left), the menu appears (right) and is readable and easy to follow.

If you use a template-based web-hosting service, your website will automatically be responsive and you will be able to add accessibility tools such as alternative text for images as metadata without needing to code. Whichever provider you choose, you need to make sure it supports HTML5, which is the new web coding standard and allows for features such as directly embedded videos (rather than requiring a plugin such as Adobe Flash).

There are many providers of template-based websites, but here are four of the most popular. All four provide template-based drag-and-drop content builders and all support HTML5. This section is intended to give you an overview of what's out there and doesn't go into full detail about each provider's features; if you're interested in more in-depth comparisons, there are plenty of resources available online. When choosing a provider you'll need to take into account your organisation's needs in terms of storage, bandwidth, functionality, user-friendliness, support and cost.

WordPress.com

The most important thing to understand about WordPress is that it can refer to two different things. In a nutshell, WordPress.org is a development tool, whereas WordPress.com is the whole package, including hosting and domain name—you can think of it like a car engine versus the entire car.

- WordPress.org—the car engine—is open-source content-management software. You can use it to build your website, which you then upload to a server of your choice (self-hosted). You'll need to buy a domain name through a third-party provider. See Chapter 5.2 for more on hosting and domains.

- WordPress.com—the whole car—is a web-hosting service powered by WordPress software and is primarily designed for blogs. Your site is automatically hosted on WordPress.com servers, including a custom domain if you choose, and all your content is stored there.

WordPress.org requires more technical knowledge than WordPress.com but is more flexible. Both versions use templates, but only WordPress.org allows 'plugins' (extra features that can be added onto your site), although WordPress.com does come preloaded with some basic plugins, such as those that allow you to create a contact form. WordPress.org allows you to monetise your site (through ads) or an online store, whereas WordPress.com does not allow you to include advertising unless you reach 25,000 pageviews per month, and even then your ad revenue will be split 50/50 with Automattic, WordPress.com's parent company.

However—and this is a big one—if you use WordPress.org you're responsible for all your own back-end maintenance, such as having spam controls, keeping regular backups and optimising your site for search engines. WordPress.com, on the other hand, takes care of all of this for you. For this reason, WordPress.com is probably a better choice for community organisations that don't have in-house technical expertise and can't afford to pay for design or ongoing maintenance.

The basic plan on WordPress.com is free; however, additional features, including a CSS (cascading style sheets) editor, domain mapping, domain registration, removal of ads, website redirection, video upload, and storage upgrades are only available on paid plans. Google Analytics is only available on a higher-level business plan, although there are other basic inbuilt analytics tools. WordPress.com is also not as user-friendly as some of its competitors, although it does have extensive support, including forums, online resources and live chat or email with the support team. It also has an app that allows you to update your site from your smartphone or tablet.

SquareSpace

Unlike WordPress.com, SquareSpace allows you to create an online store as part of your website. It also allows you to install multiple templates on a single site. Its template designs are modern and clean, but most of them are built on strong visual elements, which means you'll need access to high-quality images (either your own or stock photos) to really make them look good.

SquareSpace plans start at US$5 per month, although you can undertake a 14-day free trial initially to see if you like the platform. Support includes forums, a support centre, live chat and 24/7 email support.

Wix

Wix provides a separate mobile editor so you can directly edit the mobile version of your site, but this is because its templates are not responsive. It also has an App Market that lets you purchase add-ons to your site. Even its lowest-level paid plan includes access to Google Analytics, which is only available in higher-level plans with some other providers. Wix is also optimised for web designers working on client sites, meaning it has a higher level of functionality than some competitors. However, once you choose a template you can't change it without rebuilding your entire site, whereas other providers like WordPress.com and SquareSpace will automatically migrate your content to a new template, meaning nothing will be lost (although you may have to tweak the layout).

The basic plan on Wix is free. Wix support does not include live chat but does include email, forums and phone (although due to time differences the latter may not be as useful for users outside the United States).

Weebly

One advantage of Weebly is its mobile app for both iOS and Android, which allows you to update your website on the go. It was originally designed to build small sites for novice users and is therefore more intuitive than some of its competitors.

Weebly's basic plan is free; however, you can only create up to five pages on a free plan or up to ten on a Starter Plan (US$7 per month), which doesn't make for a particularly large or functional site. Weebly provides a support centre, forums and email support but no live chat.

5.2. Domains, hosting and custom email

Many of the web-hosting sites outlined in Chapter 5.1 also allow you to purchase a domain name through them, and will automatically host your site on their servers. Many of them also provide custom email attached to your domain. However, if you've decided to self-host your website or you want to register a domain name that isn't available through a web-hosting site like WordPress.com (for example, country-specific domains such as .com.au or .org.au) you'll need to organise your domain, web hosting and/or email separately. Many providers can give you all three as a package, and some can also help you with web design.

Domains

Computers identify websites by unique IP (internet protocol) addresses, which are a string of numbers separated by dots, e.g. 192.0.78.24. Because it's impossible to remember the IP address of every site you want to visit, domain names were created, which are words associated with a particular site's IP address.

Your domain name forms a major part of your organisation's branding—it needs to be intuitive, informative and easy for users to find. When you register a domain you're effectively leasing it for a set period; you don't own it outright. First, you need to check that your desired domain is available. This is best done through a search on a domain registrar, which will check the official domain name registry, rather than just doing a web search or typing it into your browser bar.

There are many domain name registrars, which are third-party companies that allow you to register a new domain, renew an existing registration or make changes to your domain name record. You can often purchase web hosting, domain registration and custom email from the same supplier. GoDaddy is the largest of these and provides registration services in various countries. Others may be country-specific.

Some types of domains have particular requirements for registering them. For example, if you wish to register a .com.au or .net.au domain name you need to be an Australian commercial entity with an Australian Business Number or Australian Company Number, while .org.au domain names are reserved for non-profit organisations. Other countries have similar restrictions, so check with your local domain registration body. In Australia, this is the Australian Domain Name Administrator. It's also important to check that the provider you choose is accredited with your local domain registration body to ensure quality of service.

Once you've registered your domain name, you'll need to 'point' it to the server where you're hosting your website. How you do this will depend on whether you're using a web-hosting site like WordPress.com, SquareSpace or Wix, or whether you're self-hosting, so it's best to look up online instructions for your particular platform or contact your web host.

Note that you don't have to use your domain name straight away—you can register it and let it sit while you develop your website. It's a good idea to register the domain name(s) related to your organisation as soon as possible to avoid them being taken by others. You may choose to register more than one domain (e.g. the .com and country-specific versions if you're outside the US) and point them both to the same site, so that if a customer mistypes (e.g. .com instead of .com.au) they'll still end up on your website.

There are a few things to consider when choosing your domain name. In particular, the following things should be avoided:

- **Slurls.** These are domain names that unintentionally have a double meaning, often crude or sexual, arising from when combinations of words can be viewed in several ways. The term is a portmanteau of 'slur' and 'URL'. An example of a slurl is a British fabric company, La Drape, which has the unfortunate web address www.ladrape.co.uk.

- **Long names.** If your domain name is too long it will hard to remember and type, and will also be difficult to fit on promotional material like business cards or posters. If you plan to attach an email address to it you also need to take that length into account. The maximum length you can have is 63 characters (which is extremely long); 12-13 is the average, which has gone up over time as shorter domain names have become harder to get. The main thing, however, is that your domain is memorable and easy to spell; if this is the case then length is less important.

- **Alpha-numeric names.** Names that are a mix of letters and numbers are very difficult to remember. Stick to letters only.

- **Duplicated or confusing letter sequences.** Try to avoid having a domain where the last letter of one word is the same as the first letter of the next, as it's hard to read. Your domain name should be easy to spell and easy to communicate verbally.

- **Incorrect spelling.** Check and double-check that you've spelled your domain correctly before you confirm your registration as it can be difficult to change.

- **Trademark conflicts.** Check the relevant business name and trademark registers before you register your domain to ensure you're not infringing someone else's property.

Web hosting

A server is a computer, device or program dedicated to managing network resources. Web hosting providers rent out server space for you to place your website on. This is where all the files that make up your website reside. When someone tries to access your website, their computer (known as a client) sends a message to your website's server asking for these files, which are then returned by the server to the client.

There are different types of web hosting available depending on your needs and budget. These are the main ones to consider:

- **Free hosting.** Sites like those outlined in Chapter 5.1 provide free hosting for basic services. There are also other free web hosts, such as Byet Host, that provide hosting without any of the design elements, which are useful if you've coded your own site and are just looking for somewhere to place it. The trade-off for most free hosting is ads that run on your page, and you'll also usually be allocated a sub-domain under the host's site, e.g. www.yourblog.wordpress.com. If you want to use your own domain you'll have to purchase a plan and/or pay to register your own domain. You'll also have limited control over your site's code and styling (HTML and CSS).

- **Shared hosting.** Shared hosting is where you share a server with the provider's other customers. This makes it more affordable as the cost is also shared; however, because the space is shared the server will be slower. For small websites, however, this probably won't matter too much.

- **Dedicated hosting.** With dedicated hosting, you have a server all to yourself. This improves performance and security, but it can be expensive because you bear the entire cost. This is more appropriate for larger organisations with resource-intensive sites or which require increased security.

- **Collocated hosting.** In this model, you purchase your own server located in the web host's facilities. This gives you total control (and responsibility) over the server, but the downside, apart from the cost, is that you need the technical expertise to maintain it.

Custom email

Whichever way you choose to develop your website, you should also get a custom email linked to your domain. Having a custom email address for your organisation (e.g. info@yourdomain.com) and/or for individuals is much more professional than relying on your committee members' personal addresses as points of contact. It also ensures consistency when your organisation's management changes.

There are many custom email providers that will map accounts to your domain, which you can then access through an email client such as Microsoft Outlook. However, the most popular provider at present is Google Apps, which gives you access to a custom email account using Google's standard Gmail interface and also to Google's other products such as Drive (cloud storage), Calendar and Docs (file sharing). The cost structure of Google Apps is on a per user basis, which makes it easy to add extra email addresses if needed. You can also use your organisation's Google account to sign in to third-party sites that accept Google for registration. If you're using

Wordpress.com or Squarespace and choose to get a custom email through them, it will be a Google Apps account. Although the account will look like a standard Gmail interface, the address will be your domain name, not @gmail.com.

When choosing an email address, you need to think about it in the same way as choosing a domain name. Your address should be clear, easy to spell and communicate verbally, and not too long. Also be aware that, if you're creating a mailing list, some mailing list clients like MailChimp won't let you sign up with 'role-based' addresses such as admin@yourdomain.com or info@yourdomain.com, as they often cause high rates of spam (it is still possible to use such an address in MailChimp, but it involves a work-around where you sign up with a personal email and then transfer the account's ownership to your role-based address).

5.3. Website content

This section discusses the strategy and planning behind website content, because in web writing the usability of content is just as important as the information it contains. Techniques related to the craft of web writing are discussed in Chapter 9.2.

Differences between online and print content

One of the most obvious differences between online and printed or physical content (such as books, newspapers or magazines) is the way readers consume the material and interact with the content. Physical materials are typically read front to back, with the reader taking time to absorb the content. Web-based content, on the other hand, can be viewed in a variety of ways: on a computer (in a workplace, at home, or in another environment such as a café), on a tablet or phone, or on an e-reader, and the way the reader absorbs the content is actually quite different.

In 1997, when the web was just starting to become widespread, researcher Jakob Nielsen identified a pattern as to how users read web content. His conclusion:

> They don't. People rarely read Web pages word by word; instead, they scan the page, picking out individual words and sentences.

> Jakob Nielsen, How Users Read on the Web, 1 October 1997

What Nielsen means by "scanning" is that users will first read the page headline and possibly the summary, then they'll scan across the page in two parallel stripes to find anything of interest, such as keywords, before scanning down the left-hand margin to pick out things like subheadings. Nielsen identified this "F-shaped pattern" by tracking web users' eye movements as they read. This scanning also occurs extremely quickly. Nielsen notes three major implications for writers:

1. Users won't read your text thoroughly.

2. The first two paragraphs must state the most important information.

3. Start subheads, paragraphs, and bullet points with information-carrying words.

> Jakob Nielsen, F-Shaped Pattern for Reading Web Content, 17 April 2006

This discovery went on to inform best practices for writing for the web. Specific writing techniques for web-based content are covered in Chapter 9.2. Before you start writing your content, however, you need to do some planning. This will help you identify your content's audience, purpose and timeline.

Know your reader

This is a similar process to the brainstorming about audience you've done in your strategic communications plan. Basically, you need to think about who is going to be reading your content.

- What are their demographics?

- What do they want to get out of your website?

- Why are they accessing it?

- Are they likely to be browsing or looking for something specific?

- Are there any literacy, linguistic, cultural or disability issues that may impede their access?

- How good is their physical access—are they in regional or remote areas with slow internet speeds (in which case the site may be slow to load if it contains lots of multimedia content)?

A useful tool for thinking about your users is the 'persona'. Personas are archetypes of your users—as well as identifying their characteristics, you can give them personality and make them memorable. Ideally your personas need to be backed up with some sort of research about your target market. Don't assume that your users think like you, as this could lead to you including too much assumed knowledge in your content. Keep your personas as a reference guide, and when you're writing or updating your content think about whether your personas would understand it. There are several things your persona should include:

- A generic picture of what this person may look like

- A name

- Age

- Marital status

- Family

- Location

- Life goals

- What they want to get from your organisation and your website specifically.

There are several ways you can get information to inform your personas. Firstly, talk to your users or people who interact with them. For community organisations, this may involve surveying your members, or people who attend your events or otherwise interact with your group. Ask them what they want from your website, what they think its strengths and weaknesses are, and how it compares to your competitors' sites.

A second method is to check your website analytics—the data about who is visiting your page and what they're doing while they're there. These can give you some ideas of your users' demographics, what pages they visit, where they're from, and the bounce rate (how quickly they leave the page or site). You can also attach a short survey (two to three questions) to your website to ask users about why they visited and what they want from the site. Analytics will let you see what pages the users are visiting and what pages they're leaving, while surveying your users may help give you an idea of what's missing. All this information will help you flesh out your personas.

Think also about your users' context of use—where they're using your website, when, and what device they're using it on. Are they looking for a particular piece of information or a certain product? Knowing what they're looking for can help you tailor the content to fit.

- **Where?** You need to know exactly where they are. Where they're accessing it (e.g. at work, commuting, at home) will change how much time they have to access your content and also how amenable they are to it (if they're commuting, for example, they may be tired after work).

- **When?** You need to know the peak times (day and time) they're accessing your site. You also need to know what times people are looking at specific pages and pieces of content. This information is available on your analytics tool.

- **Which device?** People will be using not just laptop or desktop computers but also smartphones and tablets. Analytics will tell you what devices people are using. There are many different types of tablets and smartphones, each with slightly different settings, so you need to be able to identify the most popular ones that people are using to access your site and optimise your content for those.

Know your organisation

As a content creator, you need to balance your stakeholders' organisational goals (e.g. to increase event ticket sales) with user objectives (e.g. to easily buy tickets). Both parties need to be catered for and their needs and goals considered. Occasionally there might be some conflicting needs, so you need to be able to educate your stakeholders about what the users need.

Ask yourself who your stakeholders are and what your business objectives are. Even as a volunteer organisation, you should have business or organisational objectives written down. These may not be financial, but they should outline the organisation's purpose and what it wants to achieve. Your stakeholders will vary depending on your organisation, its size and how formally it's structured, but possible stakeholders include:

- Governing committee/board

- Marketing or publicity manager

- Treasurer or finance manager

- Membership secretary or other person who deals directly with users

- Managers of other channels (e.g. your organisation's social media accounts)

- Subject-matter experts (this is particularly important if you're not an expert in the content you're writing about)

- Other vested interests (someone who might have an opinion about the process).

It's important to get your stakeholders on board early. What are these people's goals? What do they want to get out of the website? How will the website affect their business, e.g. will it increase their workload? What improvements would they like to see? What does success look like for them? In their idea of success, what does the content look like and how do users interact with it?

Make sure you meet regularly with your stakeholders to keep communication open, and give them plenty of lead time if you need them to check something.

Understand the purpose of your content

Your overall website must have a purpose that makes it useful to the user—it could be to inform, to entertain or to offer a particular service—but you must also understand the purpose of each page and sometimes sections of each page. If a piece of content lacks a purpose it won't be useful to the audience. Possible purposes include:

- Persuasion (convincing the user to do something)

- Information

- Education

- Entertainment

- Behavioural change (getting the user to act in a different way)

- Compliance enforcement (e.g. government websites).

Always make the user the priority—write for them, not for yourself. Use your personas to make sure that each piece of content is addressing their needs. Do a 'so what' test—the 'so what' or underlying implications of your content should be immediately obvious.

Make your content accessible

Accessibility is vital to good web design. You need to think about how you can make your content accessible to disabled users. Disabilities that could affect the way users access your material include vision, hearing or motor impairment; colourblindness; and cognitive impairments such as dyslexia.

There are some general principles that web writing should adhere to in order to make it accessible to the widest group of people. These are discussed in more detail in Chapter 9.2. The World Wide Web Consortium, which is the body that oversees the web's technical and editorial standards, also has a lot of accessibility resources.

- Leave enough white space around your text. This will make it easier for the reader to scan and will draw their eye to the most important information.

- Clearly label your links, subheadings and menus. Many websites no longer underline hyperlinks, but they should be in a contrasting colour to your text. Your menus should be intuitive and easy to navigate. Your page navigation should be logical (so users don't get caught in a loop where links continually transfer them between the same few pages).

- Your content should be 'chunked', or broken into paragraphs based on topics. You should have only one topic per paragraph. Chunking content improves scannability.

- Your headings and text should be left-aligned, not justified. This makes it easier to read, especially for people with dyslexia (see below).

- Use correct structural/semantic mark-up. This means that, for example, in your website's HTML code, the most important headings should be tagged <h1>, the next level <h2> and so on. Using structural mark-up correctly will allow devices like screen readers to properly interact with your website, as screen readers read the HTML and then translate the site's labels into spoken language for the user. If the HTML is used incorrectly the screen reader won't be able to read it. Using proper structural mark-up also improves search engine optimisation (see Chapter 5.5 for more on this).

- Check that users are able to 'tab' through your site (using the tab key to navigate links rather than the mouse) in a logical way. This is very important for users with motor impairments, who may not be able to use a mouse.

- Use inclusive language. Your organisation should already be doing this across their print materials as well as online.

In addition, there are some specific things you can do with your multimedia content and text to make it more accessible to those with disabilities.

- **Images.** Alternative text (known as alt text) is text that can be included in a website's HTML code to describe images for visually impaired people. Depending on your website's platform or content management system, you may need to include the alt text directly into your code, or you may be able to attach it as metadata to your image (e.g. in WordPress templates you can add alt text directly to the image's metadata without needing to know how to code). As well as using alt text, you could also include a description of the image as part of your content, which a person using a screen reader would be able to access. It's also important to avoid making your content (such as headings or quotes) into an image, because vision-impaired users won't be able to access it. Your alt text should be clear and succinct, and not repeat information that is already in the content.

- **Videos.** Videos that include audio need to be captioned. You can also include a transcript of your video, which has the added bonus of improving your search engine optimisation.

- **Podcasts.** Like videos, podcasts on your site should include a transcript.

- **Colour and contrast.** Although it's difficult to make a site completely colour-accessible due to the wide variety of colourblindness, there are ways to improve the usability for this group of people. Any function that is vital to the user accomplishing their goals on the site must be accessible. Your content should be presented in monochromatic colours at opposite ends of the saturation poles (e.g. black text on a white background). Navigation, such as menu bars, should be easily distinguishable from content. Contrasting colours or colours at opposite ends of the colour spectrum are the most accessible for colourblind users. Page elements such as buttons should also have a second cue other than colour (such as a distinctive shape or an image). The US Department of Health and Human Services' usability portal is an excellent resource for information about accessibility and includes a specific section on colourblindness.

- **Text and spacing.** Dyslexic users may experience visual distortion effects, which can be exacerbated by poor layout. Things to avoid to make your content more accessible to dyslexic users include justified text (which is harder for everyone to read than left-aligned text, but may cause particular problems for people with dyslexia); double spacing after full stops/periods; pure black text on a pure white background (use very dark grey and off-white instead); long unbroken paragraphs (this is generally something to be avoided in web writing in any case); serif fonts; and italicised text. The UX Movement user experience blog has an excellent resource on improving accessibility for dyslexic users.

- The 2010 and later versions of Microsoft Word, Excel and PowerPoint have an accessibility checker, which highlights any obvious accessibility issues in your text.

The Web Accessibility Evaluation Tool is another great way to check your site's accessibility. This includes a contrast checker for checking if your colour usage is accessible to colourblind or vision-impaired people.

Test your content with users

Testing your content with your users can give you insights into what you're doing well and what needs improving. Depending on your target group, you can set up an informal test (e.g. asking your members to tell you what they like and dislike about your website), which is a cheap and easy way of testing your content. At the opposite end are purpose-built facilities and specific recruitment of users. This method is more statistically sound and is often used by businesses, but it will be out of reach for most volunteer groups because it can be time-consuming and expensive, and really needs to be conducted by experts.

Review and maintain your content

It's not enough to just put your content on your website and forget about it. Outdated content or a website that has obviously not been updated for some time will make your organisation appear disorganised and unprofessional. It's particularly important to regularly update content that has a clear shelf-life, like forms or event listings.

The easiest way to maintain your content without it becoming an overwhelming task is to break up your website into sections and review them one by one. Every piece of content needs to be reviewed regularly (e.g. every six or 12 months). Having a plan or structure for auditing your content will help you go through it systematically. You may also be able to outsource different pages to different people for review, although if you do this it's important to have some sort of quality control in place to maintain consistency.

Develop a longer-term content strategy

As well as regularly updating your existing content, you need a timeline for adding new content. Regularly adding new content helps with search engine optimisation (because search engines prioritise new content) and keeps your website relevant.

When developing your content strategy, you need to think about what you're going to create (e.g. blog posts, articles, news), how it fits with your organisation's goals and business plan, and, importantly, who is going to do it. Unfortunately, content doesn't create itself, so if you're going to add, for example, one news article per week, you need to work out who's going to create it and set deadlines.

A lot of the content you create for your website will be able to be repurposed for your social media accounts, so your website content plan should be created in conjunction with your social media strategy and external communications strategy. For details on how to create and implement these strategies see Part 1.

Develop content governance policies

Although this is more applicable to businesses, content governance policies can also help volunteer organisations keep their websites organised, up to date and accountable.

A content governance policy details who owns your content and is responsible for maintaining it. If you have a team, you may give particular pages or pieces of content to different people to manage (e.g. media releases, marketing material). Write down who owns each piece of content and what they're responsible for, so that everyone is clear. It may be that some people are responsible for particular pieces of content but you or another person must sign off on it before it goes live. Your governance document needs to detail this. This allows your content to be maintained and allows for accountability.

There are two major types of accountability structures:

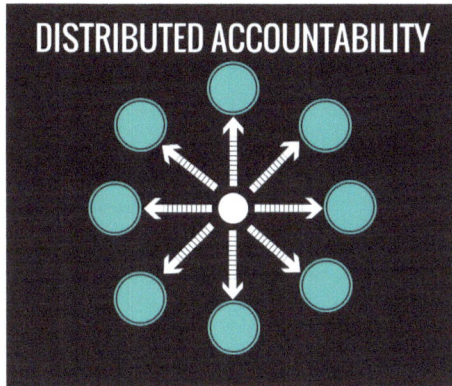

DISTRIBUTED ACCOUNTABILITY

Distributed accountability—the content is outsourced to a number of different people (probably subject-matter experts) and those people have ultimate authority to sign off on their specific pieces of content. This allows content to be approved quickly but can lead to inconsistencies if the different experts don't adhere to the organisation's style guide.

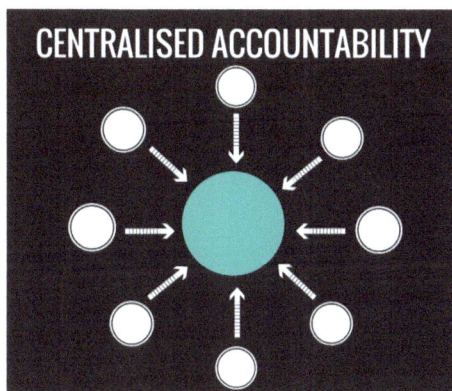

CENTRALISED ACCOUNTABILITY

Centralised accountability—all content must be approved by a central authority (usually a web or communications team/manager) before it goes live. This allows for standardisation and quality control but can also lead to bottlenecks.

All your content, regardless of who manages it, should have the following qualities, and this should be made clear to all the people responsible for updating it.

- **Timeliness:** It needs to be current and up to date
- **Accuracy:** It needs to have sufficient research behind it and be fact-checked and error-free
- **Authority:** It needs to be credible and someone needs to be accountable for it
- **Quantity:** There needs to be enough of it
- **Quality:** It needs to adhere to high standards
- **Relevance:** It needs to meet your users' and business's needs.

You also need to find a way to maintain consistency, whether that's by using a style guide, having a single person approve the final content, or both. Your website also needs to be consistent in tone and voice with other channels your organisation uses, such as email newsletters, text messages or social media. Chapter 9.5 takes you through how to create visual and editorial style guides for your organisation.

5.4. Blogs

A blog (short for 'weblog') is a regularly updated site written in a conversational style. Blogs originally started out as online diaries written by individuals, but many businesses now also use them to regularly update their users with information about the latest happenings in their industry. A blog is displayed as a series of posts, usually in reverse chronological order (newest first). Blogs also usually have a comment function where users can reply directly to the post.

Blog posts are generally quite short (usually around 500 to 1500 words) and are usually written in a conversational, informal style. Like all web content, they need to be either useful, entertaining or both. Many business posts use lists (e.g. '10 ways to improve your search rankings') as a way of conveying information quickly and easily. Other, more personal blogs, like those written by public figures such as authors, may give some insight into the writer's personality or creative process and function as a way to develop a relationship with readers.

Having a blog on your site is a very effective way of maximising your search engine optimisation (SEO), as long as it's updated regularly. Although there are lots of free sites where you can host your blog—Blogger and WordPress being two of the biggest—it's a good idea to have it attached directly to your site (e.g. yourdomain.com/blog) as any hits on your blog will also count towards your main site's SEO. If you build a site on WordPress.com, you'll automatically have a 'posts' page that you can use for blogging (if you don't want to use it, you can elect for it not to be published).

The main purpose of a blog is to build relationships with your users. You want to encourage interaction, although it's important to also moderate the comments section so that any offensive comments or users can be blocked. You can also interact with other bloggers in your field to develop relationships and possibly share links or guest post on each other's sites.

The main thing to remember about blogs is that they need to be updated regularly, so starting one is a long-term commitment. Only get into blogging if you really enjoy it—it shouldn't feel like a chore, and if it does, your readers will be able to tell. But if you enjoy writing and developing communities, a blog can really enhance your organisation's website.

5.5. Search engine optimisation

A search engine is a program that allows users to find content on particular websites by entering a keyword, phrase or subject. The most-used search engines on the English-speaking web are Google, Yahoo! and Bing (there are also other language- and country-specific search engines, such as Baidu in China). Some websites also have their own internal search engines, which only search that site. Search engines use algorithms to determine the relevance of content and then rank those results according to popularity.

Search engine optimisation (SEO) is a collection of methods and techniques that aims to increase the number of visitors to a website by ensuring that the website appears high on the list of results returned by a search engine.

There are many different kinds of SEO techniques, and in recent years there has been a proliferation of companies specialising in SEO. However, due to cost factors, most volunteer organisations will probably need to do this themselves. It's important to remember that SEO needs to be ongoing—search engines change their algorithms, so you can't just do one thing and then forget about it—and you may not see results instantly. Particularly if your website is new, it may take months to climb the search rankings.

You need to have some goals for your SEO, which means you need to be able to track what works and what doesn't. The best way to do this is through analytics, so ensure you have analytics enabled for your site (whether that's through Google Analytics or another provider) so you can see any spikes in traffic.

Keywords

Keywords are words that users are likely to put into search engines when they're looking for your page. For more detail on incorporating keywords into your content, see Chapter 5.3 and Chapter 9.2. Note, however, that keyword density (the number of times certain keywords appear on a page) is no longer a significant metric in SEO. Your content should, first and foremost, sound natural and be easy to read.

You should incorporate keywords into the following parts of your site:

- **Page title.** This is the title of the page that appears in the browser tab. Having keywords in here is the single most important thing you can do to maximise your SEO.

- **Page headings.** These should explain clearly and succinctly what the page is about.

- **Links.** Search engines favour these over normal content. Use keywords in your links rather than saying 'click here', which doesn't tell the user or the search engine anything about the link.

- **URL.** Make sure you've got keywords in the page identifier of your URL (the part that comes after the main domain name). Use dashes rather than underscores to separate words in a URL, as search engines see these as spaces and will identify the words separately.
  e.g. www.pureartscommunications.com/services/editing-and-proofreading

Content and usability

There are several ways you can design and write your website content to be more SEO-friendly:

- **New content.** Including recent content will boost your ranking in search engine results, as search engines prioritise content they haven't scanned previously. Blogs are great for this.

- **Natural language.** Using language that users actually use (e.g. 'game' as well as 'match') will help you identify keywords, and will also make your site more readable for your users. Ultimately your users are the ones who interact with your site, and the more of them who do, the better your rankings will be. So prioritise your users' experience.

- **Topical content.** Include content that is relevant to current events (e.g. the Olympics; a national election).

- **Unique content.** Try to make sure your content is something that people can only find on your website.

- **Shareable content.** Write content that is likely to be shared and linked back to by other sites—especially trusted editorial sites such as major newspapers. Having high-quality links to your page from trusted sources will improve your SEO enormously—but resist the temptation to pay for links or engage in other similar practices (the search engines are wise to this and will penalise you for it).

- **Clear design.** Ultimately, your site should be designed for your users, not for search engines. Your site should a clear hierarchy and text links, with at least one in-text link for every page. Your alt text should also be clear and up-to-date.

- **Text as text.** Search engines are still not very good at reading non-HTML text that is embedded in rich media such as images, videos, audio or Flash files. So if you've got keywords that you really want indexed (such as the name of your organisation), make sure they're contained in the actual text of your site as well as in rich media such as a logo.

There are lots of online resources regarding SEO, many of which become quite technical. If this sounds entirely foreign to you, don't worry. As long as you keep your users as your top priority and design and create content for them using their natural language, you'll automatically improve your SEO. Your content needs to be strong, accurate, accessible and based on users' needs. Identifying and incorporating your keywords and updating your content regularly are the simplest and most effective things you can do to maximise your SEO without too much cost or effort. For a more-detailed overview of SEO, check out *The Beginners' Guide to SEO* in the Further Reading section of this book.

5.6. Analytics

Analytics is data about traffic to your website—such as how many people are visiting, where they're from, which pages they visit, how long they stay, where they've been referred from, and the conversion rate (how many users achieve your goal for them, such as buying a product or filling out a contact form). Analytics data is useful for improving your search engine optimisation by showing you what keywords users are putting into search engines to find your site, and also for determining the effectiveness of your marketing—you can run a marketing campaign with specific goals, such as getting more people on your mailing list, and then use analytics to see if it has worked.

Depending on which provider your website is with, you may have basic analytics data already built in, but Google Analytics is the provider preferred by most websites.

Google Analytics

Google Analytics is a service offered by Google that allows you to monitor traffic to your website. It is the most widely used website analytics tool. The basic package is free, although there are also paid packages that offer more in-depth resources.

Although Google Analytics is free, your website provider may not support it, especially if you're using an all-in-one provider such as Wordpress.com or Wix rather than building your own site. For example, both WordPress.com and Wix only support Google Analytics as part of their paid plans, although they also have basic analytics tools built into all their plans.

Google Analytics provides basic high-level data on its dashboard, as well as reports that give more in-depth information. Your website profile can also be linked to a Google AdWords campaign to integrate your analytics and marketing.

Other providers

Wikipedia has a comprehensive list of other analytics software providers and the cost of their packages.

Analytics can provide you with important insights into your site's performance and the effectiveness of your overall marketing and communications strategy. If you're serious about improving your organisation's outreach, you need to ensure you have access to an analytics tool and learn how to use it effectively.

5.7. Google AdWords

AdWords is Google's online advertising platform, and where it generates the bulk of its revenue. It allows advertisers to display ads to users based on keywords and cookies that link the advertising copy to the advertiser's website. These ads take a number of different forms, with the most common being 'search campaigns' that appear at the top of Google's search results (with a small 'Ad' banner next to them) when a user types in keywords that match. Search campaigns are useful if people are likely to be searching for your product, service or organisation in Google.

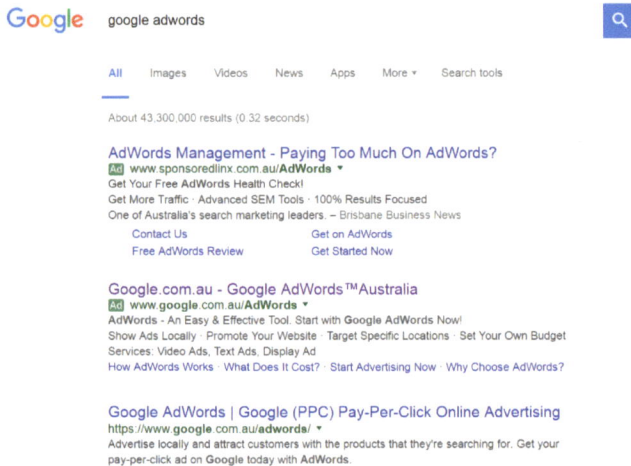

If you're running a search campaign, you need to make sure you're clear about what you want users to do once they've clicked on your ad, and that your ad copy contains your most effective keywords. Your ad should also comply with your overall marketing strategy and messages.

In your AdWords account you can track different types of 'conversions'—how people behave after they view your ad. These include:

- Online enquiries/sign-ups/completed orders

- Clicks on a link or button

- Installations of an app, or in-app purchases

- Sales/transactions/revenue/e-commerce

- Phone calls to a number listed in an ad or on a website

You need to make sure the Conversion Tracker is optimised in line with the goal of your ad so you can see if how effectively your strategy is working. In addition, AdWords can be integrated with Google Analytics so that you can also see what people who are directed to your site from your ad do once they get there.

The other types of AdWords ads are Display Campaigns, where banner ads are displayed on relevant websites, and Remarketing Campaigns, which tag visitors to your website and target them with advertising to get them to return. Display Campaigns may be useful for some volunteer organisations if you're not well known or have a new service or event that you'd like to publicise but which people are unlikely to search for directly. There are also Video Campaigns, which get your videos shown in the top of YouTube search results (although you should only use this campaign if you have a professional-quality video and if doing so will fulfil a tangible objective). However, for most volunteer organisations, search campaigns will probably be most useful. Click-Winning Content has a useful article detailing the pros and cons of each type of campaign.

Cost

AdWords operates a number of different cost structures, including pay-per-click (PPC), cost-per-click (CPC), cost-per-acquisition (CPA), and cost-per-thousand-impressions or cost per mille (CPM). In all of these variations, you only pay for results (i.e. when people click on your ad). You are also able to set your own budget, including the maximum you're prepared to spend, although you may not get the results you desire if your maximum spend is too low.

There are extensive online resources available that detail how to get the most out of Google AdWords. If your organisation is considering running a campaign, make sure you do your research and, most importantly, have an overall marketing strategy and clear goals in place before you start, so as not to waste your money.

5.8. Other tools

There are many other online tools available to make building, maintaining and promoting your website easier. Below is a short outline of some of them, although this is by no means exhaustive.

URL shorteners

URL shortening is a technique where a long web address is shortened (by creating a short redirect to the original page) to make it easier to share. It was primarily developed in response to Twitter and text messaging, where the user had to convey their message in a limited number of characters. Twitter now has its own inbuilt URL shortener, which automatically shortens any URL you include in your tweet (as well as checking it against a list of blacklisted sites), and text messages no longer have character limits, but URL shortening remains useful.

Another advantage to URL shortening is it creates a link that is easier to remember or copy from a printed document. Take, for example, the URL for my novel's Amazon page. The original URL is extremely unwieldy and full of random strings of letters, numbers and special characters:

https://www.amazon.com/Greythorne-L-M-Merrington-ebook/dp/B013QLAHVG/ref=sr_1_1?ie=UTF8&qid=1439462331&sr=8-1&keywords=l+m+merrington

Instead, I created a short URL using Bitly:

http://www.bitly.com/buy_greythorne, which is much easier to communicate to others and remember.

Some people also use URL shorteners to hide affiliate links from their sites (i.e. links to outside sites—usually used to promote products—where the original website owner gets paid when people click on the link). Affiliate links are a legitimate form of advertising, where a company pays someone with a high-traffic site, such as a popular blogger, to funnel their users to the company's product. However, disguising affiliate links—and thereby not declaring that you're being paid to spruik a product—is ethically questionable.

Aside from making links more shareable, many URL shorteners also let you track how many clicks you've had on a link, which is extremely useful if you're running a social media or online advertising campaign, as you can see how effectively your campaign is working.

There are many URL shorteners available. Some of the most popular include:

- Google URL Shortener—includes click tracking. All URLs and click analytics are public and can be accessed by anyone.
- Bitly—includes click tracking. Can be used without registering, but if you register (for free), you get access to click-tracking data (which only you can see) and you can customise your URLs to make them memorable.
- TinyURL—one of the original URL shorteners. No click tracking.
- Ow.ly—an offshoot of Hootsuite social media management software. Access to analytics only if it's integrated with your Hootsuite account.

SmartURL

SmartURL is a form of URL shortener, but its extended functionality really puts it in a league of its own. SmartURL allows you to create a single 'smart' URL that will redirect your users to the version of your site most suited to them.

For example, let's say I want to direct users to the online listings for this book. I can create a single smart URL and set parameters around it regarding country and device. This is what my readers would experience:

- User 1: Located in Australia. Accessing from a computer. Redirected to the desktop version of amazon.com.au.

- User 2: Located in the UK. Accessing from an iPhone. Redirected to iBooks.

- User 3: Located in the US. Accessing from an Android smartphone. Redirected to the mobile version of amazon.com (as this book is not available on Google Play).

The other advantage of using SmartURL is that the link you give your users will always stay the same, but you can change where it redirects to. This is particularly useful if the page you're redirecting to moves or breaks. You can simply log in and change the redirection information without having to change the link on all your marketing material or notify your users.

SmartURL also provides extensive analytics, particularly on its paid plans, although even its free plan contains click tracking and related real-time analytics.

Google Alerts

Google Alerts allows you to monitor the web for keywords of your choice. Once you've set up an alert, Google will email you articles in which those keywords feature. Alerts is a particularly useful tool for monitoring mentions of your business or organisation, especially if you're running a marketing campaign.

PayPal

PayPal is an online payments system that lets you pay online for goods and services, or receive payment for your goods and services, by linking your credit card and/or bank account. As a purchaser, it's more secure than paying directly with a credit card (and lets you pay directly from your bank account if you don't have a credit card), and as a merchant it allows you to process payments without needing a separate facility to accept credit cards. If your organisation is planning to sell merchandise or other products online, it's advisable to have a PayPal account to accept payments (you'll need to register for a business account, which will involve providing the relevant tax numbers for your country).

PayPal also now produces a card reader, PayPal Here, which works with a smartphone to allow you to accept credit card payments directly into your PayPal account without having to go through a bank. Other companies also make similar devices, like Square, which are great for organisations that don't want to have to deal in cash for membership fees or merchandise.

Online stores

If you're planning to have an online store as part of your website, you'll need to take this into account when you're building your site. Some free web-hosting sites don't support e-commerce, while others will allow plugins for third-party sites such as Shopify.

If you don't want to build a store directly on your website, a cheaper, easier option is to use a third-party e-commerce site, which will let you build your own store on their platform and then link to it from your website (for example, through a 'buy' button or plugin). There are many such providers available, but two of the most popular are:

- BigCartel—designed for artists and other creatives. Free for up to five products.

- Shopify—designed for all sorts of e-commerce. Shopify is more diverse than BigCartel, in that you can also use it in the 'real' world through their point-of-sale app and retail services (e.g. for selling goods at markets). Shopify has a 14-day free trial, but after this you have to select a paid plan.

These stores give you a dashboard that allows you to control your products, pricing (including sales) and shipping. Your customers are directed to a payment method you specify (usually through PayPal), which may or may not include credit cards. These stores make their money both from paid plans and from commissions on sales. See their websites for details of rates.

OVERVIEW

You no longer need to know how to code to build your own website due to the abundance of free template-based platforms.

When deciding how to build your website, consider how it will meet the needs of both your users and your organisation. Also consider things like budget and ongoing maintenance, and any special requirements such as an online store.

Your website must be responsive (adaptable for use on mobile devices) and accessible to disabled users.

Your domain name forms a major part of your organisation's branding—it needs to be intuitive, informative and easy for users to find.

When developing web content, think about the characteristics of your audience and also your organisation's brand voice. Your content should always be timely, accurate, authoritative, high-quality and relevant.

A blog can be a great way to build relationships with your users and give your organisation an authentic voice, but only start one if you're prepared to update it regularly.

Make sure your website employs up-to-date search engine optimisation techniques so users can find it easily.

Use analytics tools to improve your search engine optimisation and monitor the effectiveness of your marketing campaigns.

URL shorteners can help you track traffic to specific links and optimise your marketing.

Chapter 6

Traditional Media

IN THIS CHAPTER, YOU'LL LEARN HOW TO:

Understand and engage with the news cycle

Write media releases

Write opinion pieces (op-eds)

Develop interview skills for television and radio

Understand different types of media advertising

Although most community organisations will rely primarily on the internet for their communications, there is still a role for the traditional media (newspapers, radio and television), especially if your organisation focuses on trying to raise public awareness about a particular issue. This chapter will introduce several broad aspects of the traditional media: the news cycle; how to write opinion pieces for major newspapers; basic tips and techniques for radio and television interviews; and advertising in the traditional media.

6.1. Newsworthiness and the news cycle

There are two major things you need to understand before engaging with the traditional media. The first is the news cycle—the timeline on which the industry operates—and the second is 'newsworthiness', which is the criteria by which stories are selected.

The following diagram gives a basic breakdown of the news cycle.

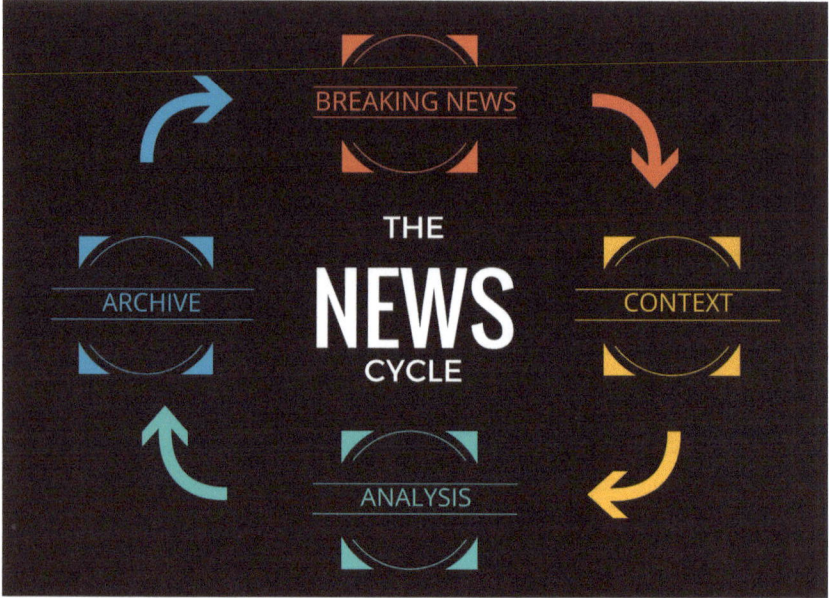

- **Breaking news:** The story is very new. Not many facts are known at this stage.

- **Context:** Within hours or days of the story first breaking, we start to learn more about what happened and the greater context of the event.

- **Analysis:** Experts start to analyse why the event occurred and what its implications may be.

- **Archive:** The story is filed away, unless new information comes to light, in which case it may be resurrected.

Many general news stories may skip the 'analysis' stage. However, stories regarding major events (such as natural disasters, aeroplane crashes or military conflicts), changes in government policy, or social issues usually have some sort of analysis attached to them.

It's at this stage that your organisation would be best placed to engage with the media. However, the time between these stages is often very short (i.e. hours rather than days), so if you see a story breaking that your organisation is in a position to comment on, you need to engage straight away. For something to be newsworthy it has to engage with current events in some capacity—and it's much easier for you to catch the wave of breaking news rather than trying to create one of your own (it's pretty rare that you'll have something that is capable of creating its own news). How and when to do this will be discussed further in Chapter 6.3, which looks at writing op-eds.

As well as targeting the right point in the news cycle, you also need to decide whether what you have to say is 'newsworthy.' If it's not, your story won't be picked up by the media. Generally speaking, your topic needs to be related to either of the following things:

- Current events

- Human interest

Can you can give a different perspective on a breaking news event that the media organisations can't get anywhere else? Think about the ways the issues of the day relate to your topic—especially if you can provide a unique insight. This is particularly applicable to issue-driven or social justice organisations.

Do you have an interesting, human-focused story that will appeal to readers/viewers/listeners? Stories about overcoming adversity are particularly powerful (which is why, for example, you see lots of variations on the story about the ordinary guy doing an ultra-marathon/swim/kayaking race to raise money for cancer research after his brother/mother/partner/baby was diagnosed). These stories will do better if you can also link them to current events, e.g. if your organisation works with war veterans, you'll get more traction around national holidays that commemorate war veterans, such as Remembrance Day or Memorial Day.

It's naturally tougher to get into the national media than it is the local media, but many community organisations are often better off targeting local media as their audience is localised. This is something you'll need to decide as part of your overall communications plan. It's also worth thinking about whether your story will appeal to a niche area of the media, e.g. the arts or sports pages of a newspaper. You'll still have to meet the newsworthiness criteria for this, but you may have a bit more leeway in specialised media.

If you're looking to publish in print media channels, such as newspapers or online sites, make sure you understand what they're looking for and what their timelines are. If they generally publish 800-word pieces, give them 800 words, not 600 or 1000. Read other pieces they've published to get an idea of the style—is it formal or colloquial? Academic or more general?

Also think about timelines—this relates back to the news cycle above. This is absolutely critical and is an area where inexperienced writers or publicists often get into difficulties. If you've got a date coming up that you'd like to publish on—such as the anniversary of a significant local, national or global event—you need to get your work to the relevant outlet at least one to two weeks in advance. They won't publish something sent to them the day before or on the day itself—it's just not possible. If you want to piggyback off a breaking news story with an op-ed, you'll need to get your article to the paper within a few hours so they can decide whether to run it the next day. Likewise, don't leave it to the week before your organisation's major event to publicise it. The earlier journalists know about something, the more likely they are to work with you.

CASE STUDY

GIVE THEM WHAT THEY WANT

A local social justice group that campaigns against the proliferation of nuclear weapons wants to use the 70th anniversary of the Hiroshima bombing to draw attention to their cause. They have great content—an interview with a survivor—but their piece is 1500 words long and academic in style and tone, and they wait until the morning of the anniversary to send it to the various newspapers they're targeting. Unsurprisingly, their piece is not picked up and their fantastic interview is wasted. Why? Because they didn't give the newspapers what they wanted: an 'inverted pyramid'-style piece of no more than 800 words, ideally provided with considerable notice—given that the date of this anniversary was known in advance, the publications would have begun planning their editions probably a month before the actual day.

6.2. Media releases

A media release is a single-page information sheet sent to news organisations to highlight an interesting story. Their aim is to encourage the journalist to find out more—they are not an end in themselves.

Not all stories are suitable for media releases, so for many volunteer organisations this will not be the best tool to use. A media release is also a bit of a blunt instrument; news outlets receive hundreds of media releases every day, so it can be difficult to get noticed. If your organisation has existing relationships with journalists (especially if you're targeting local media), a better tactic is to try to leverage these individual relationships rather than sending out a blanket media release.

You can determine if your story is suitable for a media release using the newsworthiness guidelines discussed in the previous section. Once you've chosen your story, there are a few steps you need to follow to draft a good media release.

- **Have a great headline**. This is the thing that will grab the person reading the media release. If the headline doesn't hook them in, they won't read any further. Underneath the headline, put either "For immediate release" or "Embargoed for release until (date/time)", as well as the date of issue. This will tell the journalist when they can publish the story.

- **Identify the 'so what?' factor.** In your lead, tell the reader what the story is and why they should care.

- **Put all the essential information in your opening paragraph (who, what, why, when, how).** This is the 'inverted pyramid' writing style (see Chapter 6.3 for more detail on this).

- **Identify your source(s).** Tell the reader how you know what you know. This gives your story credibility.

- **Include pictures.** Journalists love visual media, as it really enhances stories. You could also include one picture in the media release and then a link to a website where the journalist can get other pictures and/or high-resolution versions.

- **Write in Plain English** (discussed further in Chapter 9.1). Avoid jargon and make sure you've proofread it before sending.

- **Include quotes.** Quoting someone with authority gives your story credibility, colour and personality. Quotes also make it more interesting by giving readers someone to connect with.

- **Give enough information** for the journalist to be able to see the story they're going to write. Bullet points can be a good way of summarising what they need to know.

- **Provide contact details** (at minimum, an email address and a phone number, both business and after hours) at the very bottom. The journalist needs to know who to call if they want to follow up, so your contact person should be someone who is available at short notice, will respond promptly and is able to discuss the story in further detail. At the end of the release, type 'ENDS' so that the journalist knows they don't have to look for another page.

The body of your media release should be essentially written like a short news story. Learning to write a strong media release takes practice, and there are lots of in-depth resources out there to help you. But the most important thing is to ensure you've selected a strong story in the first place.

6.3. Opinion pieces (op-eds)

Opinion pieces, or op-eds (so called because in print newspapers they traditionally sit opposite the editorial page) can be a valuable part of your wider communications strategy. Op-eds in mainstream newspapers get incredible reach—far more than you could afford if you were to try to buy the same kind of advertising space (for example, if the daily reach of a syndicated newspaper in Australia is around 800,000 people, your op-ed in that publication would have the advertising equivalent of around A$20,000). In addition, unlike interviews with journalists, they're generally only lightly edited. They give you a chance to bring relatively complex topics into the public arena, and are also a good way of generating follow-up from other media outlets. They also get read by people who matter, including businesspeople and government departments and ministers, so if it's your organisation's aim to influence public policy then they're a particularly good tool.

That said, for many community organisations op-eds will be neither a necessary nor a desirable part of your communications strategy. Because op-eds work best when they can link into current events or give some sort of call to action, they're most useful for issue-driven or social justice-focused community organisations. If you're running a local sports team or community band you probably won't really need to write op-eds, unless something comes up (like a change in community arts grant funding, for example) that has a serious impact across your sector and your organisation finds itself needing to bring an urgent issue to wider public attention.

Selecting a topic

Op-eds should only be one part of your overall communications strategy, and as such they don't need to contain everything about your topic. Resist the temptation to try to include everything you know or make it overly complex—think of it as a small, self-contained piece of a much bigger puzzle.

So, bearing in mind that an op-ed topic should be relatively contained, how do you go about choosing one? The first thing to think about is newsworthiness. We discussed newsworthiness in broad terms in Chapter 6.1, but there are some more specific steps you need to think about when you're contemplating writing an op-ed.

So what makes a topic newsworthy?

- **Timing.** What is happening right now? Events from two days ago are old news. It's all about right now. Time is of the essence—otherwise you risk missing the boat. Bear in mind that newspapers plan their editions early.

- **Novelty.** Events out of the ordinary have a greater effect, so emphasise what is new or unusual about your story.

- **Personalisation.** Readers love human interest and individual stories. Use individual case studies where possible.

- **Relevance.** How strongly does the audience identify with the topic? Make it about something the reader can identify with and feel empathy for.

- **Continuity.** A story that is already in the news has its own momentum. Piggyback on existing stories or major events.

- **Clarity.** Stories with clear implications are better received than those open to more than one interpretation. Don't try to do too much. Make a strong argument, even if this means de-emphasising some of the nuances.

- **Composition.** Stories must compete for space, so if lots of people are writing on your topic it will be harder to get selected. Learn how to write a good op-ed, stick to the word count and be timely. Editors love things they don't have to work very hard for. If they realise they'll have to do an extensive edit to make it publishable they won't bother. Respond immediately to all communications and be reliable. Editors always want things five minutes ago.

The second thing to consider in selecting your topic is authority. Op-eds are written by people with some sort of claim to expertise in the area they're discussing. You can think a bit laterally about this—'expertise' doesn't necessarily have to mean formal qualifications.

CASE STUDY

FINDING YOUR EXPERTISE

Expertise can be experiential, as well as formal, and many people—especially those who've been involved in a field for a long time—often know more than they think they do. Sometimes it just requires a bit of creative thinking, but the most important thing is to make sure you always link the issue you're discussing back to your specific experience or area of expertise.

With this in mind, how could the coach of a junior football team be 'qualified' to write about drugs in sport?

As it happens, this particular club has been trialling a drug education program with its young players, with considerable success. So when a high-profile football doping case hits the media, the local coach is able to respond quickly with a positive op-ed about how they're combating drugs both on and off the field.

Learning to choose an appropriate topic and frame an effective argument is the most difficult part of writing op-eds, but it's something that you'll get better at with practice.

Structure

Op-eds are structured very differently to traditional essay or academic writing (the kind of argument writing most of us learned at school or university).

OP-ED WRITING

Lead/hook:
Most important information
and main argument

Body:
Supporting points and
evidence

Conclusion:
Reiterates main
argument

ACADEMIC WRITING

Intro:
Lays the
foundation

Evidence:
Builds argument with
lots of supporting
research

Conclusion:
Draws it all together and lays
out overall argument

As you can see, op-eds use the 'inverted pyramid' structure, where the bulk of the argument occurs at the start of the piece. The author offers their conclusions up front and then sets out evidence for how they reached them. In academic writing, the opposite is true—the introduction sets out the premise of the article, then various points of evidence are given, before finally the conclusion is stated.

Word count

Op-eds are usually 700 to 800 words in length, although different publications will have different standards. The easiest way to determine this is to read several op-eds from the publication(s) you're planning to pitch to in order to get a feel for their standard length.

Determining your argument

Before you start writing your op-ed, you need to be able to summarise your argument in a single sentence. Op-eds are built around an 'arguable statement': something that calls for evidence, either to uphold or rebut it. For example, 'The current government's inadequate funding for the arts is harming Australia's cultural life.' With this statement, you're looking to argue two things: firstly, that the current funding is inadequate, and secondly that the lack of funding is causing harm.

This argument can then be folded into your lead.

Lead

A strong lead needs to have a news hook. A good hook should immediately engage the reader—anecdotes can work well in this regard—and it should be clear about what you're arguing.

To determine your news hook, test your argument against the news values discussed above: timing; novelty; personalisation and relevance; continuity; clarity; and composition. Your story should meet all of these to be sufficiently strong.

Topic sentences

A topic sentence is a sentence that expresses the main idea of the paragraph in which it occurs. In the case of op-eds, because news paragraphs are so short, the main idea discussed in the topic sentence may cover two or more paragraphs. The topic sentence itself doesn't have to be long. In an 800-word op-ed, you want one major argument and a few (probably no more than five) sub-points to back it up.

Evidence

'Evidence' has quite a broad definition in op-eds. It is not just formal or empirical evidence, such as statistics, but also quotes from experts or authorities, precedents or examples that support your position. For example, in the arts funding argument discussed above, you could compare statistics to look at how funding has decreased over a period of time, and quote arts professionals and cultural leaders about the impact this is having (such as no longer being able to tell Australian stories). If you're part of an organisation with experience in this area (Australian arts) you would probably have enough credibility to make your own argument without needing to quote others.

Editing and proofreading

If at all possible, get someone with some experience in media writing to edit your work before you pitch it to media outlets. At the very least, your article should be proofread by another person to check for spelling and grammatical errors.

Pitching an op-ed

So once you've got a great op-ed, how do you pitch it to media outlets? Below is a step-by-step process for pitching your op-ed. Only pitch to one outlet at a time.

Although some major publications pay for op-eds, many won't, and even those that do won't pay very much. Unfortunately, it's best to think of this as outreach for your organisation and don't expect to be paid (but by all means ask!).

- **Read the publication.** Know what their expected word count is (usually no more than 800 words) as well as their style and tone. Don't exceed the word count. If it doesn't meet their standards they'll either cut it from the bottom up or just refuse it altogether.

- **Email the op-ed editor with a Word attachment.** Their addresses can usually be found online. Keep your email short, explain who you are and include a one-sentence summary of your piece. Essentially, you need to tell them why they should care about your story and why you're qualified to discuss this topic.

- **Follow up.** Give them two days, then call or send it somewhere else (send a courtesy email informing them you've moved it on). Sometimes you won't get a response, so don't wait too long, especially if your piece is contingent on current events. If they want it they'll usually get back to you quickly.

- **Have a good author photograph that's at least 400 pixels wide.** This allows the newspaper's graphic designers to work with it, e.g. manipulate the background.

- **Ask for permission to republish it** so that you can use it on your organisation's website and social media. If you get permission at the time of publication you'll save yourself the effort of having to chase it up later. Most media outlets are fine with republishing work as long as it links back to the original.

General tips

- Read the kinds of publications you want to write for and the types of articles you want to write—for tone, style and subject matter.

- Op-eds can be commentary. Just find a hook and make sure you have sufficient authority to comment.

- Be succinct—have only one, or at most two, main points.

- Avoid jargon and acronyms—imagine you're explaining your topic to a drunk friend who needs everything spelt out clearly for them (but don't be patronising).

- Have a clear opinion. Don't vacillate.

- Have a local angle where possible—for example, in Australia the news media is quite parochial, and only big topics can get by without an Australian angle. Local media will want a local community angle.

- Leverage key events and milestones.

- Embrace quirky topics.

- If you've got a topic that you know will be in the news at some point (e.g. refugees), have an op-ed body ready to go and just add a relevant introduction and conclusion when the time comes.

- Don't underestimate your expertise. 'Expertise' can also be experiential, e.g. if you're a female actor, you're qualified to write about issues affecting women in the arts.

- If you haven't done much of this before, start small, e.g. reputable blogs, then move to mainstream papers.

- Don't read the comments that appear on news sites under your article!

6.4. Interview skills for television and radio

Radio and television interviews can be daunting if you've never done them before as, unlike print, you're talking directly to the audience. In all three mediums, however—radio, television, and print—it's important to be concise and to get your point across clearly and succinctly. When preparing for an interview, write down the two or three main points you wish to emphasise and keep them in front of you to make sure you stay on track.

If you can become what journalists call 'good talent,' you're likely to be asked back; you may even become their go-to person for commentary on that particular issue, as journalists would much rather work with someone they know to be reliable than take a risk on someone new. So what makes someone 'good talent'?

- You always reply to journalists' communications promptly.

- You understand that journalists are working to very tight and often conflicting deadlines, so you're flexible.

- You always keep appointments and deadlines, and if you have to pull out of the interview due to extenuating circumstances, you always try to recommend someone who can take your place.

- You have a clear idea of the points you want to emphasise during the interview, and you get these across succinctly, but without being rude or abrupt.

- You're articulate and use language and tone appropriate to your audience. You don't dither or use lots of 'ums' and 'ahs'. Your pace is not too quick but not too slow.

- You're able to explain complex topics in ways that non-specialists can understand easily.

- You speak with passion and enthusiasm.

- You're humble and easy to work with, not a diva. You remember that this is a two-way relationship, and they're doing you a favour as much as you're doing them one.

- In short, you're professional at every stage of the process.

These guidelines all sound pretty basic but, speaking as a former journalist, I can tell you that many interviewees fail to meet them. The ones that do follow these will go straight to the top of the journalists' lists, which, if you're trying to get exposure for your organisation, is where you want to be.

CASE STUDY

THE INTERVIEWEES FROM HELL

In my experience, there are three extremes of interviewee that are particularly irritating to journalists.

The Rambler. This person is often a subject-matter expert and assumes that everyone is as interested in the nitty-gritty details of their work as they are. They're unable to see the forest for the trees: rather than giving the main overarching points (which is generally all a journalist has time or space for, and if they want more detail they'll ask), they go off on all sorts of tangents, speak in fragmented sentences, drone in a monotone and are generally thinking about themselves more than the audience. For the journalist, it's particularly awkward having to interrupt them constantly to bring them back on track. If they're being interviewed for recorded television or radio (as opposed to live), their failure to speak in full sentences and their tendency to drone on and on makes them a nightmare to edit.

The Root Canal. This person takes 'concise' to mean 'monosyllabic'. When the journalist asks a question, they answer it in just a few words—or, worse, with just 'yes' or 'no'—and won't elaborate unless pushed. Even these elaborations are abrupt. For the journalist, getting information out of this interviewee can feel like pulling teeth—they're having to pour a lot of energy into someone who is giving very little back. Although it's important to be succinct, what journalists are looking for are people who can join the dots: take their question, answer it, and then link it to other interesting information that they wouldn't necessarily have thought to ask about. The ideal interviewee knows their topic inside out and is able to make those analytical leaps quickly, but still expresses them in a way that's easy to understand.

The Politician. This is the interviewee with an agenda. Career politicians are notorious for doing this—often dodging or refusing to answer questions that don't fit their talking points—but anyone who is looking to push an obvious agenda falls into this category. It's one thing to work with the journalist to get your points across in a calm, considerate manner; it's quite another to push your agenda at all costs. Interviews like this often end up getting quite adversarial.

No matter what kind of interview you're preparing for, do your research. Know a bit about the radio station/television station/newspaper and especially who their target audience is. Look up the interviewer and see what other work they've done. The better prepared you are, the more comfortable you'll be.

Don't worry if you slip up or make a mistake—just correct it and move on. Often these things appear bigger to you than they actually are, and the audience may not even notice. Also don't be afraid to admit you don't know something or that it's not really your area—it's far better to do this than make it up and end up giving incorrect information. You can also shift the discussion if it's going a way you really don't want it to: "I can't give you that information off the top of my head, Sarah, but what I can tell you is…"

Afterwards, email the host or station to say thank you—it's good manners and it's always useful to maintain good relationships with journalists. You can also ask them for an audio or video clip of your segment to use on your organisation's website.

Radio

Radio is a highly personal medium, because you're talking directly to listeners, and more often than not you'll be live rather than recorded. It's often more colloquial in tone than television, especially if you're on talkback radio. The lack of visuals means you're relying entirely on your voice to give a good impression and get your point across, because the audience can't see your body language. You also don't have time to go into complex, long-winded explanations or a lot of detail: the audience needs to be able to grasp your message easily first time around. That said, don't overthink it. Talk to the interviewer naturally or you'll come across as stilted and nervous.

Most radio interviews will be conducted by phone, as it's easier than getting you into the studio, especially if the station is not in your local area. Make sure you arrange the phone interview for a time when you won't be interrupted, and go to a quiet place with no distractions. If you've been asked to call them at a certain time, make sure you're prompt. Alternatively, a producer will call you about five minutes before the interview is due to start, and you'll be placed on hold until they're ready for you. While on hold, you'll be able to hear the radio show. Don't have the show playing on your own radio in the room with you—many programs have delays on their broadcast (usually around seven seconds), and this creates a strange audio feedback loop if it's heard over the phone during the interview.

Smile while you're talking—this will make you sound more enthusiastic. Standing up during the interview will make you feel more confident. Keep a glass of water nearby in case your mouth gets dry.

Television

Television has an added dimension to radio, in that your body language matters. You need to present as credible, professional, open and engaging in your dress, general deportment and the way you interact with the interviewer (who is a proxy for the audience).

- A dress tip: avoid patterns like checks or stripes, which tend to 'pop' or render oddly on screen. Go for plain, bold colours that enhance your skin tone.

- Don't look at the ceiling if you need time to think.

- Use deliberate, controlled gestures and take a moment of silence if you need time to gather yourself, rather than using filler words like 'um'.

- Slow down your speech. You'll naturally talk a bit faster if you're nervous, so you may come across as babbling.

- Pretend the camera isn't there and talk directly to the interviewer. If the interviewer isn't appearing in the shot (as in most news interviews), they'll usually stand to one side of the camera to ask their questions. Look at them, not directly down the camera, as this comes across as 'breaking the fourth wall' and is disconcerting for the viewer. Maintain eye contact with the interviewer.

When preparing for a television interview, it's a good idea to do a filmed mock interview with a friend or colleague. You don't have to have fancy equipment—you can even film it on a phone. But filming it is important because people often react quite strongly to the idea of being filmed and get distracted or speak much more haltingly than they normally would. Watching yourself on video, you'll also notice any odd tics or gestures that you use habitually, such as tugging your hair or fiddling with jewellery, or any off-putting body language.

6.5. Advertising

For many volunteer organisations, advertising in the traditional media will be both unnecessary and prohibitively expensive. However, if you do decide that media advertising is a route you'd like to explore further, there are some options available.

Advertising goals

Before you engage in any advertising, either in the traditional media or online, you need to have a firm idea of what you want those ads to achieve. For example, do you want it to lead to increased ticket sales to your play or sports match? Do you want to gather new members? Are you aiming for greater overall brand recognition? You also need to work out how you will measure success—is it financial or something else? Your goal needs to be quantifiable so that you can decide whether this kind of advertising is something you wish to continue pursuing in future. This needs to be a conscious decision based on facts, rather than just throwing good money after bad because you have a gut feeling it's helping.

You also need to set a budget and timeframe that will give you the best chance of reaching your goals without straining your organisation's finances. Depending on the arrangement with the media outlet, this may include the cost of producing the ad itself as well as running it. In general, radio is the best medium for community organisations in terms of affordability and reach, and radio ads are quick and easy to produce.

There are many resources available about how to produce effective ads for different types of media, but it's also a good idea to talk to people in the industry. For example, if you decide to advertise on local radio, talk to them about the most effective strategies for developing your ad. Many radio stations also offer package deals where production of the ad is included. Just make sure you undertake effective planning and research before you commit to any sort of advertising to ensure you get the best value for money.

Regional media

The cost of advertising in national newspapers, radio and television will place this out of reach for most volunteer organisations. However, it's worth considering your local or regional media, as these will be more affordable and will also target people in your local community. Your options in this regard will depend a lot on where you live. In Australia, which is the market I'm most familiar with, the media is highly concentrated. The major metropolitan newspapers, television and radio stations are split between a few large corporations and two public broadcasters, and these same corporations also own much of the regional media. In other countries, such as the US, the regional media market is much more diverse, so you will have more options. It's worth finding out about your local media, including their reach (how many people read them?) and demographics (who are those people?) to see if they fit with your communications strategy.

Community media

Many places still have vibrant community media organisations (which are mainly staffed by volunteers). Radio is a particularly popular community medium because it has a wide reach with lower production costs than either newspapers or television. Although the reach of community stations will not be as wide as commercial or publicly funded local media, their audience demographics may suit your organisation's purposes. Community media audiences are often highly engaged with their local communities and keen to become involved. As always, do your research first, not only into the audience but into the media outlets themselves, as some may not take paid advertising.

OVERVIEW

The news cycle—breaking news, context, analysis, and archive—is the timeline on which the media industry operates. Knowing how your story fits into the news cycle will make it easier to engage media interest.

Your story also needs to be 'newsworthy'—generally related to either current events or human interest.

Characteristics that make a topic newsworthy include timeliness, novelty, personalisation, relevance, continuity, clarity, and composition.

Make sure you give journalists plenty of lead time, especially in relation to events.

A media release is a single-page information sheet sent to news organisations to highlight an interesting story and encourage journalists to find out more. They must be engaging in order to stand out.

Opinion pieces (op-eds) can be a valuable part of your communications strategy, but they work best when they can link into current events or give some sort of call to action. Consequently, they're most useful for issue-driven or social justice-focused community organisations.

Op-eds must be written in the 'inverted pyramid' style and are usually no more than 800 words in length. They must include a lead, topic sentences and evidence.

When being interviewed for radio or television, be concise and to get your point across clearly and succinctly. Write down the two or three main points you wish to emphasise and keep them in front of you to make sure you stay on track.

Before you engage in any advertising, either in the traditional media or online, you need to have a firm idea of what you want those ads to achieve. You also need to set a budget and timeframe that will give you the best chance of reaching your goals without straining your organisation's finances.

Regional and community media may offer better advertising options for volunteer organisations than national media outlets.

Chapter 7

Social Media

> ### IN THIS CHAPTER, YOU'LL LEARN HOW TO:
>
> Use Facebook, Twitter, Instagram, Snapchat and LinkedIn
>
> Understand other social media sites
>
> Use social media management tools

The proliferation of social media networks in recent years means that it's now extremely difficult for a group or organisation to maintain a presence across the majority of networks. With this in mind, this chapter outlines the major social media networks and their current demographics and reach, to allow community groups to choose which networks best serve their purposes. This chapter concentrates on the social networks that are most popular in the West; if your target market is elsewhere, particularly in Asia, there are other region-specific networks that you will need to investigate.

In general, it's best to have a strong presence on one or two networks rather than spreading yourself too thinly across many. Social media works best when it's regularly updated, which means that most volunteer organisations won't have the time to develop a strong presence on more than two networks.

There is a misconception that social media can be used as a direct-marketing tool to drive sales of a product or service, or membership of an organisation. However, social media is primarily relational and is best used for interaction and community-building. You may not see a direct increase in sales or membership as a result of a social media campaign; however, if you can develop a strong online community you will increase your organisation's visibility and word-of-mouth, which will have an indirect impact.

The demographics and statistics listed here were correct at the time of writing, but given how quickly social media changes, it's worth doing your own research if you're looking to target specific demographics.

With all social media, it's imperative you understand the relevant privacy settings, especially regarding personal accounts. In short, know who will see what you post. This also goes for location settings—many networks allow you to 'check in' to a location or use metadata from your photos to detail where they were taken. This can have privacy implications, so if you're not comfortable sharing your location, make sure you know how to disable it.

For more details on how to develop social media posts, see Chapter 9.3.

CASE STUDY

CHOOSING YOUR SOCIAL MEDIA NETWORKS

Most volunteer organisations won't have the need or the resources to be on every single social media network. It's far better to do one thing well than many things badly. The network(s) you choose will depend on your audience.

There are two football clubs servicing the same general area of around 50,000 people. Club A's committee has heard that it should have a social media presence, so it has created a Facebook page, a Twitter account and an Instagram page. However, it hasn't developed any guidelines for these and the person who is meant to be maintaining the accounts is often too busy to keep up with them all. Consequently, the content on the Facebook page is out of date, the Instagram page is basically inactive and the Twitter account is used periodically, but the posted content doesn't always fit with the club's stated values as a family-friendly organisation.

Club B, in contrast, has a clear social media strategy. The committee has decided to focus on Facebook, because its audiences are adult players and the parents of junior players, who use Facebook as their primary form of social media. The club has developed a public page where it posts regular updates about matches, information for fans and notices of recruiting drives, and has buttons where people can send a direct message or email to the club secretary. It also has a closed group for members where training schedules, match draws and club social events are posted, and where members-only discussions can be held. This group is moderated by the committee member responsible for social media to ensure that all content and discussions adhere to the club's values and standards.

Even though Club B is only on one social network, because its audience is there too this is a much more effective use of its resources than trying to have a wide presence.

7.1. Facebook

Overview

Facebook is the grandparent of social networks, both in terms of its longevity and, increasingly, its demographics. Although Facebook strives to maintain its original image of a social space for hip young college students, its highest percentage of users is now in the 35–54 age bracket.

That said, Facebook is still the largest global social network, with over 1.86 billion monthly active users (users who access their account at least monthly) around the world as of February 2017, so having a presence here is almost essential. It's also arguably the social network with the best set-up for businesses and organisations, although a recent change to its algorithms means that just liking a page is no longer a guarantee of seeing its content. For page owners, this means that you generally have to invest in paid advertising if you want to reach all your followers.

As well as written posts (known as status updates), Facebook also supports videos, photos and links. Posts with multimedia in them tend to get a better reach than text-only posts. Facebook also now allows for cross-posting from Instagram, which it owns.

Profiles

Facebook profiles are individual accounts. They are under an individual's name and have a 'wall' where friends can post comments, photos or videos. Profiles can be set to public (viewable by anyone on the internet) or private (viewable only by people the owner has approved as friends). Individuals will see a 'newsfeed' which lists posts from their friends and any pages they follow.

Do not set up a profile for your business or organisation; Facebook will delete it, as profiles are designed for individuals. Organisations need to use pages instead (see below).

Pages

Facebook pages are designed for businesses, organisations and public figures. Although they share some of the same features as profiles, such as a wall, they also have other features such as maps showing the organisation's address and contact details, links to the organisation's website, and messaging features to allow the page owner to be easily contacted. There are also third-party apps that can be installed, like links to online stores. Page owners can also create a 'call to action' to sit at the top of the page—for example, this could be a link to a mailing list sign-up page, a petition or a website.

Individuals are able to 'like' pages, which, in theory, will allow those pages' posts to show up in the individuals' newsfeeds. However, as noted above, a recent change to Facebook algorithms means that just liking a page is now no guarantee of seeing all its posts.

Pages are set up and managed by one or more individuals—these people need to have existing Facebook profiles. You can set administrator rights in the page's settings, giving people full admin rights or lower-level permissions as necessary. Administrators are able to purchase advertising for the page and also have access to its analytics (called 'Insights'), which shows you how many people your posts are reaching and how many people are engaging with your posts (liking or commenting on them), among other things.

Although Facebook pages can be managed from smartphones or tablets through the Pages app, the desktop version provides more-comprehensive analytics data.

Messenger

Messenger is Facebook's private messaging app for smartphones and tablets (on the desktop site messages are contained within the user's profile). Messenger allows people to contact each other privately. You can change the settings on your personal profile to control who can message you (i.e. strangers or only your friends).

Messenger is also used for people to contact business pages. Facebook rewards business/organisations that respond promptly to messages by publishing their response time on their page (i.e. 'usually responds within an hour'), which makes your organisation look reliable and on the ball. Try to respond to messages as quickly as possible.

Groups

Facebook groups are places where people with common interests can gather—they're the community halls of the internet. Groups can be either public (open to anyone), closed (visible to anyone but requiring an invitation to join) or secret (visible only to those who are invited by an administrator). Groups are a useful way for community organisations to create sub-groups of members—for example, only people on a particular sports team, or involved in a particular event—or, for smaller organisations, to communicate with all their members. They provide a central repository of information, and also a space where members can post questions or comments, share information and generally interact with the rest of their community.

Administrators need to keep an eye on the group membership to make sure that people who are no longer part of the organisation are removed, and newcomers are added. It's also a good idea to post some guidelines at the top of the group's page that indicate what is and is not acceptable in terms of discussion, language use, self-promotion etc. Posts should be monitored to make sure they meet these standards and, if not, they need to be removed and the issue discussed privately with the poster. Properly moderated Facebook groups can be great places to strengthen your community, but they do require quite a bit of attention to ensure they stay civil.

Events

Facebook allows individuals or pages to create events, to which they can then invite other users. Events can be public or private, and the invitation list can be restricted (for example, in the case of a members-only party) or open (in the case of a public event where the aim is to get it shared as widely as possible). The event page will contain the date, time and location, as well as a description of the event. The description field can also be used to include links to further information, such as a ticketing site or an email address. People can respond to the invitation in three ways: going, not going, or interested. For public events, individuals can also forward the invitation to their friends.

One downside to Facebook events is that it can be harder to gain solid RSVPs, as people often don't take a Facebook invitation as seriously as a personalised invitation and may not respond.

Advertising

Over the last two years, Facebook has been positioning itself as a 'pay-to-play' platform, meaning that businesses and organisations now need to advertise in order to reach substantial numbers of people (including, controversially, their own followers, whose loyalty they have arguably already earned through unpaid means).

When you design a Facebook ad, you customise it to the needs of your organisation, nominating a targeted demographic and budget. There are three different ways to advertise on Facebook, and they all offer slightly different features.

- **Boosted post.** This option allows you to pay money for a post you've already published to be promoted more widely. It's the easiest way to advertise but also the least effective as you have only limited control of targeting and can't set an advertising objective.

- **Ads Manager.** Facebook's Ads Manager tool allows you to set an objective for your advertising—for example, clicks to your website, page likes or event responses—which will target your ad to people most likely to respond. You can also target your advertising to very specific audiences, including custom profiles that you create, and you have greater control over your budget and schedule. When used properly, this can be a very effective way of advertising.

- **Power Editor.** The Power Editor is the next level up from Ads Manager, providing all the same functionality plus extra conversion-tracking features; however, it is also the most complex to learn.

There are many good online resources about how to maximise your Facebook advertising—including how to design an effective ad—so, as with all advertising, do your research before you jump in.

The Facebook Business page is probably the best place to start, but there are also many third-party resources out there. At a minimum, you need to have a good understanding of your target audience, your advertising objective (how you want your audience to respond to your ad) and your budget. The good news is that Facebook ads are a very affordable way of advertising and, for many organisations, will be much more effective than other forms if used correctly.

7.2. Twitter

Overview

Originally called a 'microblogging' platform, Twitter is a social network where users exchange short 'tweets' of 140 characters or less. The original idea was based on mobile phone SMSs. Tweets are public by default (although users can restrict messages to just their followers) and Twitter's strengths tend to be real-time commentary on breaking events, and networking and community-building for groups of like-minded users. Users 'follow' other users, which means the tweets of those they're following will appear in their feed in reverse chronological order (most recent first).

In May 2016, Twitter announced some changes to the 140-character limit. Multimedia, such as photos and videos, the person's username, and attachments and links no longer count towards the character limit, giving users considerably more space (a photo used to count for around 24 characters).

Twitter is not the place to be if you want to reach teenagers. Twitter's users sit mainly in the 18–49 age bracket. It has 313 million monthly active users (users who access their account at least once a month), with nearly 80 per cent of its accounts outside the US. Twitter is the most popular social network in Japan, making Japan the only country where Twitter outranks Facebook.

Twitter has had problems with bots (automated 'followers' designed to make an account appear to have more followers than it actually does), with a black-market trade in these fake followers emerging. The network also has a reputation for responding poorly to abuse, although it has now instituted a 'report abuse' form after a public outcry. It is a much more public forum than Facebook or

Instagram, so if you choose to be active there you need to bear this in mind.

Twitter can be extremely powerful if used effectively, but it does require a fair investment of time. It's important to know what your organisation's aims are and whether Twitter's demographics align with your target audience before you sign up.

Hashtags, mentions and retweets

Hashtags are words prefaced by the # symbol and are used to group topics together. Users can search for a specific hashtag and read all tweets that use that tag. Mentions are usernames prefaced by the @ symbol and are used to reply to or draw the attention of specific people. For more on hashtags and mentions see Chapter 9.3.

Users can 'retweet' a tweet they particularly like by clicking the 'retweet' button. This will make the tweet visible to that user's followers.

Trending topics

Trending topics are words, phrases or topics that are being mentioned at a greater rate than other topics. This could be because the topic is particularly newsworthy, or because a group of people (such as fans of a particular celebrity) have got together to make a concerted push for popularity.

Twitter Lists

A Twitter List is a curated list of accounts (you don't need to be following an account to add them to the list). For example, if you want to follow other organisations in your industry, you could group these together so that when you click the list you will only see tweets from the accounts on that list. Lists are public by default (anyone can see the lists you create) or you can set them to private. Lists are good ways of keeping track of accounts without having to follow them, and viewing the Twitter Lists of a prominent person in your field can be a good way of finding new networks to engage with.

Periscope and Vine

Periscope is a live video-streaming app owned by Twitter and launched in March 2015. It allows you to stream video live from your phone to selected users—you can either publicly tweet a link to your live stream or restrict it to specific viewers. You can also choose whether to allow comments on your video as it streams. Periscope can be useful for volunteer organisations to live-stream events and thus get a reach beyond the physical location—just make sure you're not infringing copyright when you do so. Periscope broadcasts are recorded and remain available within the app for 24 hours after the broadcast, and they are also saved to your smartphone, enabling you to share them like any other video.

Vine is another Twitter video app that lets users capture and share short (up to six seconds) looping videos. Unlike Periscope, Vine videos are much more akin to regular tweets—short, sometimes trivial, and quite often creative or funny.

Advertising

Unlike Facebook, Twitter has proved to be an enormously difficult platform to monetise, as evidenced by the fact that, despite having existed for a decade, the company is still not profitable.

Twitter ads are structured much like Facebook ads, where you nominate an objective, target audience and budget. Twitter ads show a higher click-through rate than Facebook ads (where users click the ad), but Twitter ads are considerably more expensive than Facebook ads and have a lower reach overall just due to the difference in the numbers of people who use the platforms.

7.3. Instagram

Overview

Instagram is a popular photo- and video-sharing social network now owned by Facebook. Although it has a desktop interface, it's primarily app-based, with users taking photos or short videos with their phones and uploading them directly. Instagram was one of the first networks to pioneer photo 'filters', which are presets that change the light and colour grading of photos to give them a particular look, such as vintage or sepia. Photos can also be geotagged with their location (based on GPS coordinates).

Like Twitter, Instagram uses hashtags to group photos by theme, and mentions to allow users to interact (see Chapter 9.3 for more details on this). There are often strong communities that develop around particular hashtags, such as #bookstagram (where users upload photos of their favourite books, often with short reviews underneath). Profiles can be set to public or private, and Instagram accounts can also be connected to other social networks, such as Facebook, Twitter, Tumblr and Flickr, to allow easier sharing.

Instagram is one of the fastest-growing social media platforms, with around 500 million users. It's slightly more popular among women than men and is most popular with the under-35 demographic, coming second only to Snapchat among teenagers. Instagram is not the place to reach older users, with its popularity among the 50+ age group only just cracking double-digit percentages.

Instagram Stories

A new feature that Instagram released in 2016 was Instagram Stories, which allows users to compile multiple photos of their day into a single slideshow 'story' (rather than posting them individually) that disappears after 24 hours. This was widely speculated to be an attempt to steal ground from Snapchat, which pioneered the 'stories' feature. As on Snapchat, stories can be embellished with text, drawings or stickers. There is no public comment feature on stories, although users can send a private message to the story's author. Stories are particularly useful for cataloguing a particular time period, such as an event, without cluttering up the user's Instagram profile or spamming followers with an excessive number of posts.

Advertising

In May 2016, Instagram unveiled a suite of business features, including updated business profiles and analytics. Because Instagram is owned by Facebook, Instagram advertising is integrated with the Facebook Advertising platform and can be managed through the

Facebook Ad Manager and Power Editor (see Chapter 7.1 for more details on these). Like other social media advertising, on Instagram you select an objective (such as clicks to website), which will affect who your ad is shown to. There are three types of ad to choose from: Photo, video or carousel. Photo ads are similar to regular Instagram posts, with a single image and some text; video ads can be up to 60 seconds long and can now also be produced in landscape format; and carousel ads allow users to swipe through a series of images and also provide a call-to-action button to direct them to a website. Because Instagram is built primarily on high-quality visuals, you need to make sure your ads have really strong imagery in them, or they won't gain traction. This is important on all platforms, but particularly so on Instagram.

7.4. Snapchat

Overview

Snapchat is the current social media darling, having grown rapidly since its launch in 2011. It's primarily a private-messaging app, where users send each other photos or short videos, known as 'snaps' and often embellished with text, filters, humorous drawings, real-time special effects, sounds or stickers. Snaps disappear after a set amount of time—between one and ten seconds, depending on what the user selects—although users can take a screenshot of received snaps in order to keep them (the sender is notified when this occurs). Snapchat claims the self-deleting feature is a response to the longevity of information on social networks and its desire to provide a platform where users can interact in a more authentic way without feeling they have to curate their images to be 'perfect'. Snapchat also recently moved into video and audio calls, similar to Facebook Messenger and WhatsApp.

Snapchat is the current social media platform of choice for teenagers, with speculation that teenagers are becoming more attracted to private messaging because of having grown up with constant messages about the importance of maintaining online privacy. However, as Snapchat becomes more mainstream, its demographics are starting to skew older. Snapchat has 100 million daily active users (unlike Facebook and Twitter, Snapchat measures daily active users rather than monthly active users), and 10 billion videos viewed daily. Its users are mostly young women and girls (70 per cent) and over 70 per cent are millennials (aged under 35). Only 2 per cent of Snapchat users are aged over 55.

Snapchat Stories

A Snapchat Story is a curated selection of snaps that appear in chronological order and form a narrative. Stories can be viewed unlimited times for up to 24 hours and can be set to either 'friends' or public.

Advertising

In the last year or so, as Snapchat has grown in popularity, businesses have been scrambling to work out how best to use the platform to reach the coveted millennial market. However, unlike Facebook, Twitter, Instagram or LinkedIn, Snapchat advertising is primarily targeted at large corporations; there aren't yet any affordable options for individuals or small businesses.

Snapchat offers several different kinds of advertising:

- **Snap Ads.** These are 10-second videos that appear in the context of other snaps. Users can swipe up to see more, like longform video content, an article, app download or website link.

- **Sponsored Geofilters.** A geofilter is a location-based overlay that users can add to their snaps, like a piece of art that can be superimposed on their photos. Anyone can submit a geofilter for selection by Snapchat, but standard geofilters aren't allowed to include brand identifiers or trademarks. With Sponsored Geofilters, when a user in a nominated location sends a snap, they'll be provided with a list of geofilters they can select from, including sponsored ones. These are useful for location-oriented brands, such as events.

- **Sponsored Lenses.** Lenses are real-time special effects or sounds that users can overlay on their snaps. Sponsored Lenses are brand-oriented special effects designed to be playful and interactive. However, these don't come cheap, at between US$450,000 and $750,000 a day.

  o Snapchat also has sponsored content in its 'Discover' feature, where news organisations list selections of stories, similar to Snap Ads.

7.5. LinkedIn

Overview

LinkedIn is a business-oriented social networking platform aimed at enhancing corporate networking. Because it fills a very specific niche, its market share is small compared to Facebook or Twitter, with around 106 million active users. However, due to its professional-networking focus, it could be useful to have a presence on there if your organisation is more business-oriented, such as social justice organisations.

LinkedIn's demographics are not so much age-related as interest-specific. It's a good way to establish connections with business acquaintances that you may not feel comfortable connecting with on a less-formal platform like Facebook. The emphasis is on connecting with people that you know, or asking to be introduced to secondary contacts who work at the same company as people you know. Although you can invite anyone, if too many contacts respond to your invitation with 'I don't know this person', your account can be blocked. LinkedIn also lets you search directly for jobs, and post jobs as an organisation. Although a basic LinkedIn account is free, unlike other social networks it also offers a paid 'premium' package with enhanced features.

One criticism of LinkedIn is that it has one of the worst user interfaces of any social network. For example, when signing up for an account, it's easy to accidentally spam all your email contacts with LinkedIn invitations rather than just the ones you've selected.

Profiles

A LinkedIn profile is much more akin to a CV than a Facebook profile. It allows you to list all your skills and work experience, as well as any honours, awards or qualifications you've received. You can also ask your contacts for short recommendations on your work. You can post news or articles much as you would on Facebook, although LinkedIn posts are almost always business-related rather than personal. Your contacts' posts show up in a newsfeed on your home page, and you can interact with them in much the same way as on other social networks, by liking, commenting or sharing. LinkedIn also has a feature that lets you see how many people have viewed your profile, and who they are (unless they've set their preferences to anonymous).

Articles

In addition to posting status updates, you can also write articles for LinkedIn on a topic in your area of expertise. This can be a good way to showcase your knowledge and skills to your contacts, and is really a form of content marketing in the same way a blog post is. You need to treat this with the same level of care as if it were being published on a website or in a newspaper—make sure it's well-structured, succinct and clean (no typos). For more details on how to write opinion pieces, see Chapter 6.3.

Messages

LinkedIn has a private messaging function that allows you to send private messages directly to your contacts individually or in groups.

Company pages

As well as personal profiles, LinkedIn also lets you create a company page for your organisation (similar to business pages on Facebook). This is where you can showcase your organisation and promote your brand. The main function of a company page is to provide engaging content that is then shared with your followers.

LinkedIn supports multimedia, including videos linked directly from YouTube, and company pages also have built-in analytics.

Groups

LinkedIn offers groups where professionals from the same industry or area of interest can congregate to share tips and experiences. Much as on Facebook, users can join existing groups or create one of their own. Groups can be unlisted (by invitation only) or public, although users still have to ask to join.

Advertising

There are two types of LinkedIn advertising: Sponsored updates and text ads. Sponsored updates are displayed in the newsfeed like an ordinary post, whereas text ads are smaller and appear down the right-hand column. Sponsored updates can contain images linking to the advertiser's website or LinkedIn company page, whereas text ads are shorter and contain only thumbnail images as well as text and links.

LinkedIn ads are best suited to business-to-business marketing, i.e. businesses that provide products or services that benefit other businesses. They're more expensive than both Facebook and Twitter ads, so they need to be carefully targeted and monitored to ensure you're getting a sufficient return on your investment.

7.6. Other social media sites

Tumblr

Tumblr is a social networking site with around 550 million monthly users, where users create mini-blogs. Without text or photo limitations like Twitter or Facebook, Tumblr is a lot more flexible. It allows users to post text, audio, video, quotes, links, chat and other content and, unlike other networks, Tumblr profiles are fully customisable, either through templates, or your own designs if you can write HTML/CSS. Users follow others' blogs and can 'reblog' them in their own blog (much like retweeting on Twitter), or add comments or likes. Like Twitter and Instagram, Tumblr uses mentions to let you tag other users using @username. You can also tag your posts by category in much the same way as using hashtags on other platforms. Tumblr also has an instant messaging feature. There are a number of different advertising options, including sponsored posts and sponsored blogs. Nearly 70 per cent of Tumblr's user base are millennials (born between 1981 and 2000) and half are under 25.

YouTube

Now owned by Google, YouTube is the original video-sharing site and is still the most popular, with around 300 hours of new content being uploaded every minute and over 4 billion videos viewed every day. Users can upload, share, rate and comment on videos of up to 15 minutes in duration. Videos are viewable by anyone, but only registered users can upload. Most videos are free to view, although there are some paid subscription or premium channels. Channel owners can also earn revenue through advertising, leading to significant incomes for the most popular channels (an average of $23,000 per month for the 1000 most popular channels). YouTube videos can also be embedded on external sites, including social media profiles or blogs. Tutorials on everything from makeup to video games to home improvement are especially popular. YouTube cuts across age demographics, being extremely popular among both young and older users, although the content they're accessing differs.

Pinterest

Pinterest is a photo-sharing site that bills itself as "the world's catalogue of ideas". Rather than sharing their own photos as on Instagram or Flickr, Pinterest users curate 'pinboards' of pictures that inspire them and can interact with other users, including following the boards of those with similar tastes and 'repinning' others' posts. For example, a user may have a board devoted to recipes, another to fashion and a third to travel. The most popular categories on Pinterest are food and drink, DIY and crafts, women's apparel, home decor, and travel. Pinterest has 100 million active users, the majority of whom (between 60 and 85 per cent, depending on who you ask) are women, although its popularity is growing among men. The main age bracket of users is 25 to 34, with 35 to 44 the next-largest group. Businesses can also create Pinterest pages, which serve as a virtual storefront. Interestingly, Pinterest's referral rates to online stores are much higher than from other social networks like Facebook (i.e. if a user sees an item they like on Pinterest, they're much more likely to buy it).

Google+

Google+ (sometimes written Google Plus) is Google's foray into social networking. Although sometimes held up as a competitor to Facebook, Google+ is structured quite differently, and has nowhere near the same reach or influence. Users have a profile, similar to Facebook, but contacts can be organised into 'Circles', meaning that they can be grouped together by interest or by their relationship to the user, e.g. colleagues or close friends. The user can then choose to post only to particular Circles. The Stream, like a Facebook newsfeed, shows updates from the users' Circles. Another feature of Google+ is Hangouts, which are free video-conference calls of up to 10 people. Hangout users can use various apps to share documents or screenshots with other users. Hangouts On-Air allows for live-streaming of a Hangout to YouTube, which will also record it for later sharing. These are often used to stream events. Similarly to Facebook, businesses or organisations can create a Google+ Page, and all users can create a Google+ Community, which is an ongoing conversation on a particular topic, similar to a Facebook group. The Google+ app (although not the desktop version) also offers an Events service similar to its equivalent on Facebook, and this is also integrated with Google Calendar.

The network has around 375 million monthly active users. The vast majority (between 65 and 75 per cent) of Google+ users are men, and 55 per cent are located in the US. Interestingly, the main professions of Google+ users are engineering, teaching, web development, design and software engineering—suggesting that Google+ is still mainly populated by well-educated, tech-savvy American men. If this is your target demographic, Google+ could be a good solution for your organisation; if not, it probably shouldn't be your first choice of social network.

WhatsApp

WhatsApp is an app-based messaging service owned by Facebook. It allows you to send free text or voice calls, even internationally (because it uses your phone's data rather than voice plan) and you can also share photos, videos and documents. WhatsApp's main drawcard is that, unlike email or other messaging systems, it uses end-to-end encryption. The platform has over 1 billion users, making it the most popular messaging app.

WeChat

WeChat is a Chinese app-based social platform that combines messaging, e-commerce, gaming and social networking. It was launched in 2011 by Chinese company TenCent and has 700 million monthly active users, 90 per cent of whom are in China. The chat function is similar to Facebook Messenger or Snapchat, but it also combines voice and video calls and allows for money transfers. WeChat Moments is a newsfeed of your connections' posts, and the 'send red packet' function allows you to gift money to your connections (in line with the Chinese tradition of giving 'red packets' of money at Chinese New Year and on other special occasions). WeChat also has a 'shake' function, where you can shake your phone and connect with others all over the world who are shaking their phone at the same time—it's designed as a way of making new friends. It also has a unique function called 'message in a bottle,' where you record a short message and when someone picks it up they hear your message and can choose to respond (you can also pick up bottles from others). WeChat also includes games within the app and a banking and investment service, including the ability to pay for goods at physical stores through the app. Companies that do business in China can also create one of three types of 'official account' to promote their business.

WeChat is really the next level of social network in terms of the breadth of functions it offers. Its main user base is in China, but the app is localised in 20 different languages and contains a message translation feature as well. If your organisation is targeting audiences in China, WeChat is worth exploring.

7.7. Social media management tools

With the proliferation of social media networks in recent years, it has become increasingly difficult for businesses in particular to keep up with the demands of being on multiple platforms. In response, a number of social media management tools have emerged, which allow you to control multiple social media accounts from a single dashboard, as well as scheduling posts and suggesting content for reposting. In the case of Twitter, Instagram and LinkedIn, using a third-party tool is the only way to schedule posts for a later time, as this functionality is not available in the networks' native interfaces.

Below are profiles of some of the most popular social media management tools, although like anything social media-related, new tools are emerging all the time, so it's best to do your research to select one that best suits your needs.

Hootsuite

Canada-based Hootsuite is the most popular social media management tool, with over 10 million users. It allows users to integrate Facebook, Twitter, Instagram, Google+, LinkedIn, YouTube, Tumblr, Flickr and other social media accounts, as well as third-party services like WordPress and MailChimp, into a single dashboard. This lets users monitor feeds and schedule posts across multiple accounts easily, from both desktop and app versions (although the app's functionality is more limited). Hootsuite has also released a beta version of an analytics tool for Facebook and Twitter, which lets you compare data for all the accounts you manage. You can also monitor your streams using keywords, which is particularly useful if your organisation is in the middle of a crisis and you need to keep a close watch on what people are saying on your social media.

In addition, Hootsuite's Suggestions feature aggregates content that users can then search to find relevant content to repost. It also has an extension for the Google Chrome web browser called Hootlet, which makes it easy to share websites across your social media accounts. Hootsuite also offers comprehensive training in various aspects of social media strategy and practice through its online members-only platform, Podium.

Hootsuite has a basic free plan, with three social profiles, basic analytics and scheduling, which may be enough for a small organisation without a wide social media presence. However, to access its more powerful features, you'll need to upgrade to a paid plan.

Buffer

Although often held up as Hootsuite's main competitor, Buffer is more of a content publishing platform than a comprehensive social media management tool. Hootsuite and Buffer offer similar things, but Hootsuite provides more features, arguably at the cost of usability, while Buffer's interface is less complex and cleaner. Buffer focuses more on post scheduling and less on engaging and monitoring. The biggest difference is that Hootsuite will let you respond directly to content on your feed from your dashboard, whereas Buffer will only let you publish new content. Buffer is also better integrated with other automated scheduling tools. Buffers analytics also focus on the performance of specific posts rather than accounts overall, so if you post to your social media accounts outside of Buffer, data for those posts won't show up in Buffer analytics.

Like Hootsuite, Buffer has a browser extension and app. It may be a better choice for organisations that want to keep their social media organised but don't necessarily need the level of functionality or complexity that Hootsuite offers.

Edgar

Edgar is a social media scheduling tool that, unlike Hootsuite or Buffer, recycles content so that your accounts are always active. Your content library is sorted into categories, such as 'promotional' or 'inspirational' (or whatever other categories you choose) and you can decide when to post content from particular categories to your networks. Once Edgar reaches the end of the content list in a particular category it goes back to the start and shares it again. The upside to this is that your social media accounts are always active. The downside is that if you don't set up your content library properly or if you have too little content, Edgar will continue reposting the same things and essentially spamming your followers.

Edgar also lets you post native images to Twitter, which Hootsuite doesn't (if you post an image to Twitter through Hootsuite you'll just get a link to that image rather than the image itself). It also has a Chrome browser extension to allow you to post directly from the web. However, Edgar is significantly more expensive (US$50 a month rather than US$10 a month for the equivalent plan on Hootsuite), which may put it out of reach of many individuals and volunteer organisations.

Sprout Social

Sprout Social is a social media management platform. It is more comprehensive than Buffer in the features that it offers, in that it goes beyond simply scheduling content. Like Hootsuite, it allows monitoring of social media platforms, campaign creation and implementation, and assigning tasks across teams. It integrates with Facebook, Twitter, Instagram, LinkedIn and Google+, as well as Bitly and Google Analytics. However, unlike Hootsuite it doesn't yet allow integration of some of the less popular social networks like Tumblr and Flickr. Sprout's interface is cleaner and easier to use than Hootsuite's, but although it offers a 30-day free trial, the cheapest plan is $50 per month (per user), which only includes up to five profiles.

TweetDeck

TweetDeck is a free, Twitter-only management program (now owned by Twitter) that allows you to monitor and post to multiple Twitter accounts. Because Twitter doesn't have a scheduling tool in its native interface, you'll need to use TweetDeck or another social media management tool if you want to schedule posts on Twitter. TweetDeck has both desktop and app versions and it's free for an unlimited number of accounts (there is no paid version). However, unlike the other tools on this list, TweetDeck only manages Twitter and does not have any analytics or more sophisticated tools.

OVERVIEW

In general, it's best to have a strong presence on one or two networks rather than spreading yourself too thinly across many.

Social media works best when it's regularly updated, which means that most volunteer organisations won't have the time to develop a strong presence on more than two networks.

Social media is primarily relational and is best used for interaction and community-building rather than direct marketing.

With all social media, it's imperative you understand the relevant privacy settings—including location settings.

A social media management tool can allow you to manage multiple accounts from a single dashboard, schedule posts and share content.

Chapter 8

Mailing Lists

An up-to-date email list is one of the most powerful marketing tools community groups can employ, because it allows you to communicate directly with the people that matter most to you in a targeted way and without having to pay for advertising. In the last few years, there has been an explosion of free software that lets you curate your list, produce branded sign-up forms for your website and social media, send professional-looking HTML emails, and track the data associated with those emails, making it easier than ever to develop an email list.

Using a mailing list provider also ensures you avoid privacy issues such as accidentally putting all addresses in the 'carbon copy' (cc) field rather than 'blind carbon copy' (bcc), or other practices that may put you in violation of various countries' anti-spam legislation (such as not providing an unsubscribe facility or contact details for the sender).

In this chapter, we're going to look at this software in a bit more detail, examine how you can use mailing list analytics to improve your communication strategy, and discuss some techniques for growing your email list.

8.1. Mailing list services

Email marketing software

MailChimp is one of the best-known online email marketing software providers, although there are others that offer a similar service, such as Benchmark Email and VerticalResponse. These companies differ in the services they offer, but many have free plans up to a certain number of list recipients (2000 for MailChimp, 1000 for VerticalResponse) and a monthly email cap (12,000 for MailChimp, 4000 for VerticalResponse). You will need to investigate which software best meets your needs, and these are some things to look for in a free plan.

- **Time period:** Is it permanently free or is the plan only offered as a limited-time trial?

- **Contact numbers:** How many contacts can you have on your mailing list for a free plan?

- **Monthly cap:** How many emails can you send per month?

- **Templates:** Does the program offer HTML email templates, and how easy are they to use? Are they free or do you have to pay for them? Are they responsive (viewable on mobile devices as well as desktops)?

- **Sign-up forms:** What sorts of sign-up forms can you create?

- **Importing contacts:** Are you able to import existing lists of contacts or do contacts have to sign up individually through the software's sign-up form?

- **Multiple lists:** Can you manage multiple mailing lists through the one account?

- **Integration:** Is the software set up for easy integration with the most popular free website hosts, like WordPress? Can you access it through apps on smartphones or tablets?

- **Reply functionality:** If a subscriber wants to contact you, how easy is it?

- **Analytics:** What sort of data does the program allow you to track? Are you able to request email notifications for certain types of data (such as new subscribers)?

- **Support and training:** Does the software company offer good support and information to help you improve your email marketing?

- **Upgrades:** What do the paid packages offer, and are they affordable should you need to upgrade in future?

Analytics

One of the great advantages to using an email marketing provider is access to analytics. These are the most common data that you can track from your mailing list provider.

- **List growth.** How many people are subscribing to (or unsubscribing from) your list each month?

- **Open rates.** How many people on your list opened the email you sent them (as opposed to deleting it without reading it)? How does this compare to averages across your industry? This gives an idea of how engaging your subject line is, among other things.

- **Click rates.** What percentage of subscribers are clicking the links in your email? This indicates how interested your subscribers are in your content.

- **A/B testing.** Some providers let you run tests on two different versions of your subject line, sender name or content to see which version is the most popular. This allows you to make better-informed marketing decisions.

8.2. Managing your mailing list

Once you've decided to set up a mailing list, you need to encourage people to join. The first thing to do is create a sign-up form, embed it on your website and link it to your social media accounts. You may choose to put it as a pop-up on your website (there is a whole lot of science behind how to maximise the utility of pop-ups without turning people off) or just have it as a simple link or button. Make sure the design of your sign-up form adheres to your branding in terms of logos, colours and fonts. If you're hosting an event, you can also have an area where people can sign up directly. MailChimp, for example, has an app that lets you display your sign-up form on a tablet.

CASE STUDY

SEGMENTING YOUR LIST

Mailing lists work best if they contain like-minded subscribers (i.e. people who are interested in a particular thing). If you have a broad audience, you may want to consider segmenting your list.

A local amateur theatre group is interested in reaching two types of people (as well as its members, who have a separate list): those interested in performing with the group; and potential audience members. It initially believes these are two distinct groups, so it decides to create two separate email lists.

On its sign-up form, people are asked to fill in their name and email address and then select their area of interest from a drop-down menu (e.g. 'I am interested in receiving information on: auditions; upcoming shows; both). These people are then funnelled into the appropriate category and will only receive the type of information they want. However, if the group finds that most people who sign up to its list select 'both' (e.g. because most people who perform in theatre are also interested in watching it), it may change its approach and stop segmenting its list.

Incentives

In general, the best way to build a mailing list is by providing some sort of incentive—something subscribers can't receive anywhere else. Although it used to be enough to offer 'regular news and updates,' these days some sort of free content or other material incentive tends to work best. Many authors, for example, use a free ebook as an incentive to attract new subscribers. The amateur theatre group above could offer a voucher for one complementary ticket to its next show, valid for a certain number of months from the date of the subscription.

Although this may seem counterintuitive, it's what is known as a 'loss leader' in marketing and economics, where something is sold below its market value in order to drive sales of other related products (we also discussed this in Chapter 4.7 in relation to event promotion). In the amateur theatre example, the cost of one complementary ticket will probably be offset by future ticket purchases from that subscriber, especially since people generally prefer to go to the theatre with others, so that subscriber may actually bring along new audience members who would not otherwise have come to the show.

Whatever incentive you offer, you need to make good on it. Don't make an offer and then hamstring it with arduous conditions or otherwise make it difficult for the subscriber to claim. By giving you their contact details, your subscribers are placing trust in your organisation, and they are also giving you a very valuable marketing tool. Don't take it for granted.

Sending emails

There are a couple of different ways to manage your mailing list. You could decide to send out a regular newsletter—for example, monthly or fortnightly (weekly tends to get a bit spammy)—or you could send out news emails on an ad hoc basis, such as when you have a major event. What works best will depend on your organisation and target audience. Taking the amateur theatre group example in the case study above, it may be that a regular newsletter works best for the members-only list, while emails to potential audience members only need to be sent in the lead-up to shows.

Make sure your template is clean and easy to read, and that your content has been proofread and is properly spaced. Don't make your email too long—people's attention spans are short and their time is limited. Put your most important messages up front. The tone of your email should conform to your brand voice—for details on how to develop this see Chapter 3.2.

Embed links in your emails that subscribers can visit for further information, but avoid saying 'click here'. It should be clear where the link is going to ('click here' could go anywhere) and bear in mind that many of your subscribers will be viewing your email on a smartphone or tablet, rather than using a mouse (so not technically 'clicking'). Make sure all your links are active and unbroken before you send the email.

Send a test version to yourself before you send it to your list, so you can check the layout, design and link functionality, and check for any other errors.

Avoiding spam

You will need to comply with anti-spam legislation and your mailing list provider should have procedures in place to help you do this. Among other things, this means you will need to provide contact details, including a postal address, which will go out on every email you send. You will also need to make sure your subscribers are able to unsubscribe at any time (this is usually done through an automated link).

Remember that most people receive tens or even hundreds of emails per day, so don't annoy your subscribers by emailing them too often. If your open rates are going down and your sending frequency is high, this could indicate frustration among your subscribers with the number of emails you're sending them.

Keep your list up to date

This is a huge issue for volunteer organisations, particularly those with a lot of turnover in their membership. Although automatic unsubscribe buttons help, if you're sending out members-only emails then you need to make sure that your list is kept up to date, that new members are added, and that anyone who is no longer a member is removed. This means the person in charge of your membership needs to go through the mailing list regularly to check that it remains accurate. There's no point sending emails to people who no longer want or need to receive them, and in the worst case you may have issues with confidentiality if non-members are receiving members-only information.

OVERVIEW

An email list allows you to communicate directly with the people that matter most to your organisation in a targeted way and without having to pay for advertising.

Using a mailing list provider will ensure your emails look professional and comply with anti-spam legislation.

Mailing list analytics allow you to see how many people are reading your emails and optimise your strategies for reaching them.

Ensure your mailing list is always up to date.

Chapter 9

Writing

IN THIS CHAPTER, YOU'LL LEARN HOW TO:

Write in Plain English

Use active and passive voice

Improve cohesion in your writing

Select an appropriate voice, register and tone

Use the Microsoft Word Readability Index

Write for the web

Write for social media

Edit and proofread your work

Develop written and visual style guides

It goes almost without saying that writing is one of the most important aspects of good communication, yet unfortunately it's an area where many organisations fall short. This chapter gives you some practical tips on how to improve your writing, as well as specific sections on how to write for the web and social media. It also discusses editing and proofreading, and how to develop a style guide for your organisation.

9.1. Improving your writing

This section details some easy methods you can use to immediately improve your writing. These principles are applicable to all kinds of writing, from formal documents to writing for the web or social media. Using them will ensure your audience clearly understands your meaning without having to reread your text.

The tools outlined below are not hard-and-fast 'rules', as all writing requires the author to exercise judgement. The most important thing to keep in mind when you're writing is your audience—what will make life easiest for them? Will they be able to understand what you've written? How much can you assume they know in terms of background and also industry-specific terms? Your audience must be at the forefront of your mind in every decision you make about your writing.

Plain English

Plain English is a style of writing that is becoming increasingly popular, particularly as a reaction against business jargon or 'managerialese'. Plain English emphasises writing clearly and concisely, using commonly understood terms, in a style that is appropriate for your audience and easy for them to understand. The British author George Orwell was one of the strongest advocates of Plain English, which he detailed in his 1946 essay *Politics and the English Language*. Orwell believed that deliberately vague or obscure language—particularly that used by governments—was used to hide the truth and "designed to make lies sound truthful and murder respectable, and to give an appearance of solidity to pure wind." The essay is out of copyright and is available for free online.

Things that should be avoided in Plain English writing include:

- Euphemisms

- Jargon (industry-specific words)

- Acronyms and abbreviations (unless clearly identified on first use)

- Technical terms

- Clichés

- Words that are changing in meaning

- New words that may not yet be understood by most people (e.g. paywall)

- Old words that are no longer in common use (e.g. whilst, ought—replace with 'while' and 'should')

- Overly complex words (use a simpler alternative)

Plain English does not mean 'dumbing down' your ideas. It's possible to write about complex subjects, including technical subjects, in Plain English without losing any meaning. In fact, the aerospace and defence industries have developed their own standard, known as Simplified Technical English, which employs many of the same principles as Plain English, with the aim of reducing ambiguity, improving clarity and comprehension (especially for readers whose first language is not English) and making translation easier.

Active and passive voice

Writing in active voice is one of the best ways to get your point across clearly, and it's particularly essential in web writing or anything intended for the general public.

Active voice is recommended because it personalises the sentence and places responsibility where it belongs—we know exactly who did what. It also emphasises the actor, who is usually the most important part of the sentence (there are a couple of exceptions to this, explained below).

Active voice is one of those things that people are often told to use without being told exactly what it is or *how* to use it. In this explanation I'm not going to use the 'correct' grammatical terms because, in my experience of teaching writing, these often lead to confusion. Instead, I'm going to explain active and passive voice as simply as I can, in the hope that doing so will demystify it for you.

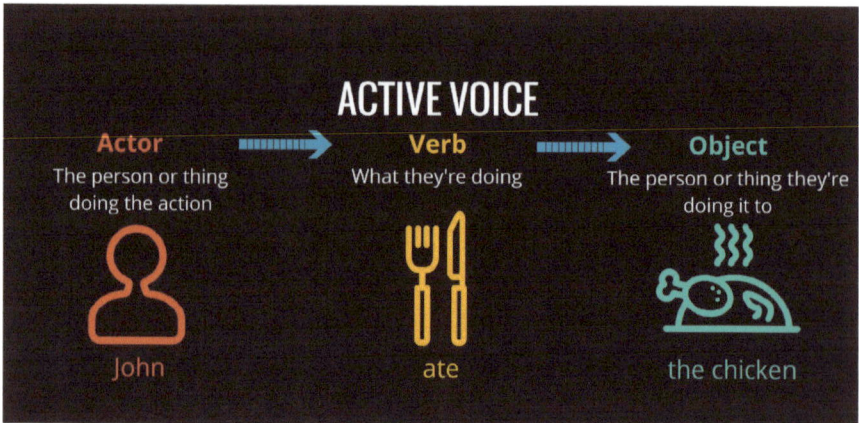

ACTIVE VOICE

Actor	Verb	Object
The person or thing doing the action	What they're doing	The person or thing they're doing it to
John	ate	the chicken

In active voice, the actor/subject always comes before the verb, because they're directly performing the action. The easiest way to check if your sentence is in active voice is to identify the verb and the actor, and make sure that the actor is before the verb.

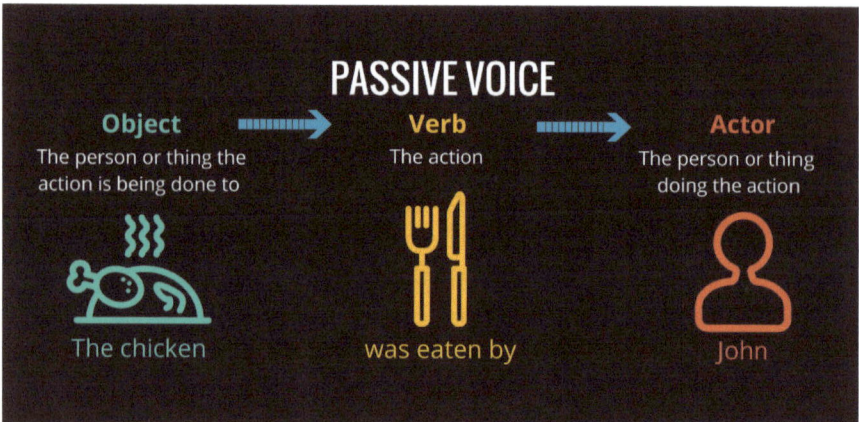

PASSIVE VOICE

Object	Verb	Actor
The person or thing the action is being done to	The action	The person or thing doing the action
The chicken	was eaten by	John

In passive voice, the actor comes after the verb. 'By' is a classic indicator of passive voice (e.g. 'The girl was bitten *by* the dog'), although not all passive sentences will use it. Again, identify your actor and your verb and check their order. It's possible to have a passive sentence with no actor at all (e.g. 'The girl was bitten'—we don't know who or what bit her), which is often used to hide responsibility (e.g. 'It has been decided that your position will be made redundant'—we don't know who made the decision so we don't know who to complain to).

Although we generally prefer to use active voice, there are two circumstances where passive voice is appropriate:

- **The actor isn't important.** E.g. 'Baking powder was added to the flour to make the cake rise.' In this sentence it's not important who added the baking powder—the important thing is that it was added and that, as a result, the cake rose.

- **The actor is unknown.** E.g. 'The club's logo was designed over 30 years ago.' We don't know who designed the logo— that information has been lost, and it's not vital to the sentence that we know.

You shouldn't try to use active voice 100 per cent of the time; if you do, you'll potentially end up with some slightly weird sentences. Documents written entirely in active voice sound unnatural, but you shouldn't have more than about 20 per cent of your document written in the passive voice or it will become difficult to read. See the section below on the Microsoft Word Readability Index for details on how to identify the percentage of passive voice in your document.

Sentence length

Keeping your sentences short is one of the best ways to improve the readability of your work. Ideally, your average sentence length across your document should be less than 25 words (see the section below on the Microsoft Word Readability Index for details on how to measure this). This doesn't mean you can't have sentences longer than 25 words, but rather that you want to keep the average down across the whole document. The reason for this is because once sentences exceed 25 words they become much harder to read (for further details on this, see the UK Government's excellent resource, *How People Read*, listed in the Further Reading section of this book).

CASE STUDY

WHEN SENTENCES GO ROGUE

Here's an extreme (real-life!) example, written by a lawyer to a doctor asking about a client's ability to work. This sentence is 104 words long.

If you consider our client is capable of undertaking suitable employment and having reference to the physical injury and giving consideration to our clients [sic] ability to work in employment having regard to the entirety of our clients [sic] personal circumstances including the injury causing incapacity and other circumstances personal to our client bearing upon her ability, not simply to perform physical tasks required by particular employment, but to work in that employment as a settled member of the workforce, is it considered that she has no current work capacity which will continue indefinitely or alternately whether she is suited to full-time or only part-time employment?

The moral of the story? If you want to be understood, keep it short!

There are a few simple ways to shorten your sentences:

- Break the sentence in two by inserting a full stop/period. If you do this, however, remember to insert some 'transitional expressions' (e.g. however, as a result, therefore, consequently) to make your sentences flow. If you don't do this your writing will become jerky.

- Cut out redundant phrases (e.g. '3am in the morning'—you can just say 3am; 'completely unanimous'—just say unanimous).

- Avoid overusing intensifiers like 'severely' or 'really'. There is no real difference between 'inadequate' and 'grossly inadequate', for example.

- Delete unnecessary phrases such as 'all things considered', 'as a matter of fact', 'at the present time' and so on. They generally don't add anything to the sentence.

- Replace phrases with a single-word descriptor (e.g. 'a large proportion of people'—'many people')

- Write according to the principles of Plain English—delete clichés, euphemisms, jargon and technical language. Most of these only serve to make your sentence wordier.

- Replace long in-text lists with bullet points, as long as doing so won't break the flow of the narrative for the reader.

Cohesion

Cohesion is the narrative flow of your document. Good cohesion is what links sentences and paragraphs together and makes the writing flow smoothly. If a piece of writing lacks cohesion it will be disjointed and difficult to read.

Cohesion occurs at both document and sentence/paragraph levels.

Document-level cohesion includes:

- **Document structure.** There must be thematic progression throughout your document.

- **Paragraph order.** They must proceed logically.

- **Introduction and conclusion.** They must encapsulate the major aspects of your document and map out or sum up your argument for the reader.

Sentence-level cohesion includes:

- **Relevance**—each sentence must be relevant to the preceding one, but not exactly the same. If there is not enough relevance the writing will feel disjointed. If the second sentence is just repeating what the first sentence has already said, it's redundant.

- **Order**—sentences within paragraphs need to flow logically and they must all relate to the main idea of the paragraph. Some ways to order sentences include: showing cause and effect; comparing and contrasting; chronological order; or clarifying (starting with a broad first sentence then going into detail in the next sentence).

- **Linking or transitional words**—words or phrases that are used to join sentences and provide flow. Examples include: however, therefore, consequently, as a result, in contrast, likewise, in short, at first, in summary.

- **Repetition of key words or phrases**—repetition can remind readers of your focus and provide clarity, but don't overdo it.

Word choice

Word choice is extremely important for clarity in your writing. Poor word choice can lead to the reader feeling that the writing is awkward, vague or difficult to read. These are some examples of common word choice problems.

- **Misused words.** The word doesn't mean what the writer thinks it does.

  E.g. 'No one is the suppository of all wisdom' (this was an actual quote from former Australian prime minister Tony Abbott)
  Revision: 'No one is the *repository* of all wisdom.'

- **Words with unwanted connotations or meanings.** E.g. 'I'm sorry I'm late; I was waiting for an escort.'

Revision: 'I'm sorry I'm late; I was waiting for someone to escort me through security.'

- **Using a pronoun when readers can't tell whom/what it refers to.**

  E.g. 'My sister cried when my mother went overseas, because she loves her a lot.'

  Revision: 'My sister cried when my mother went overseas, because she loves Mum a lot.'

- **Jargon or technical terms.** Write to inform, not impress. Writers sometimes drop in jargon because they think it makes them sound 'smart,' when in fact it has the opposite effect. Only use technical terms if they're absolutely necessary.

- **Loaded language:** The writer assumes a term is commonly understood and relies heavily on it without defining it.

  E.g. 'Working families,' a slogan used throughout the 2007 Australian federal election but never properly defined.

- **Redundancy:** Using a long phrase that can be encapsulated in a single word, or using the same collection of words over and over.

  E.g. 'In the event that…'

  Revision: 'If…'

- **Clichés, slang and colloquialisms:** Words and phrases that are appropriate in speech often sound too informal in written documents. They can also lead to misunderstandings, as not everyone will know what they mean.

  E.g. 'When writing, avoid clichés like the plague.'

  Revision: 'You should avoid using clichés in your writing.'

Reading your work out loud can be a good way to check for poor word choices. It will especially show up any redundancies. Always get someone else to read your work before you publish it, as you'll often miss your own mistakes. See Chapter 9.4 and Appendix D for more editing resources.

Voice

Writing voice is the writer's unique way of expressing their personality, which comes across in the word choice, register and tone that they use. Everyone has their own writing voice, but in marketing and communications terms brands also have a 'voice'. If you're writing something in your organisation's voice, it means taking on the characteristics that you've decided best encapsulate your brand (such as playfulness or authority) and modifying your tone and writing style to communicate these.

It's important that your organisation's voice remains consistent across all its communications—whether physical publicity materials, email newsletters, web content or social media posts. For this reason it's good to have one or two people sign off on all content before it's published, especially if it's been written by several different people.

Register

Register is the style of language or level of formality used in your document. It varies from casual to highly formal. The register you choose will depend on your audience, the purpose of the document and the brand voice that you want to communicate.

- **Casual:** What's up?

- **Informal:** Hi

- **Neutral:** Hello

- **Formal:** Good evening

- **Highly formal:** How do you do?

In web writing, we usually use the informal register, as web content is generally a bit more casual than physical documents. See Chapter 9.2 for more detail on this. Newspaper articles usually use a neutral register, while official letters or invitations may range from formal to highly formal. The main thing is to choose a register that's appropriate for your document and audience. If in doubt, especially when writing letters or emails to someone you don't know, it's best to err on the side of formality. Your organisation's marketing content should all be written in a consistent register.

Tone

Tone is the attitude of the writer towards a subject or audience. It could be friendly, dismissive, informal, standoffish, casual, aggressive or neutral (or many others). When writing on behalf of your organisation, it's important to choose a tone that reflects your organisation's values and brand. Also be aware that writing can sometimes sound more abrupt or aggressive than speaking because the tone is often not as subtle or as easily understood. Likewise, sarcasm and humour can sometimes be difficult to distinguish in written form—so much so that there's an internet maxim known as Poe's Law, which states that, "Without a winking smiley or other blatant display of humour, it is utterly impossible to parody a fundamentalist in such a way that *someone* won't mistake [the parodied view] for the genuine article."

Tone is shaped by your word choices and sentence structure. One-sentence paragraphs, for example, may sometimes seem a bit abrupt. As tone will directly affect the emotional reaction the reader has to your writing, it's extremely important that you make sure you're communicating your message in the way you intended. If in doubt, ask someone else to read it for you.

Microsoft Word Readability Index

The Microsoft Word Readability Index is a tool built into Microsoft Word that gives you metrics relating to the readability of your writing. Readability is a measure of how easy it is for your reader to understand your writing straight away. You want good readability because it will allow you to reach a wider audience and will ensure your audience understands your writing the first time they read it. Using the principles outlined above—Plain English, active voice and short sentences—is the best way to improve your readability.

The tool calculates readability by using an algorithm based on word length and sentence length. Note that it doesn't measure structure, logic, tone, register, cohesion or any of the other elements of good writing, so it's still possible to have a poorly structured, illogical document with good readability.

To turn on the Readability Index: File > Options > Proofing > check 'Show Readability Statistics' box. Run the spellcheck and your readability statistics will appear after the spelling and grammar has been checked.

There are four main things to look for in the readability statistics:

- **Average sentence length:** Less than 25 words.

- **Percentage of passive voice:** Less than 20 per cent.

- **Flesch Reading Ease:** Between 50 and 60 for more formal documents; between 60 and 70 for web writing and writing intended for the general public. This is a measure of how easy your document is to read. The higher the number, the easier it is to read. A document with a score of 60 to 70 should be easily understood by a 14-year-old.

- **Flesch-Kincaid Grade Level:** For more formal documents, 10 to 12. For web writing and writing intended for the general public, 8 to 9. This is a measure of how many years of formal education your reader needs to understand your writing.

CASE STUDY

READABILITY EXAMPLES

Here are some examples of readability statistics from my own writing.

This is from a formal document, written in a legalistic tone. As you can see, the sentences are overly long, there's a relatively high percentage of passive voice, the reading ease is quite low, and the grade level is quite high.

Readability Statistics	? ✕
Counts	
Words	1367
Characters	6894
Paragraphs	16
Sentences	42
Averages	
Sentences per Paragraph	3.8
Words per Sentence	31.9
Characters per Word	4.9
Readability	
Passive Sentences	28%
Flesch Reading Ease	37.3
Flesch-Kincaid Grade Level	15.2
	OK

The second example is from the introduction to this book, which I've tried to write in Plain English. The average sentence length is still a bit on the long side, but is within the recommended length; the percentage of passive voice is very low; and the reading ease and grade level are about right for this book's intended audience.

Readability Statistics ? ✕

Counts
Words	890
Characters	4602
Paragraphs	20
Sentences	36

Averages
Sentences per Paragraph	4.5
Words per Sentence	19.4
Characters per Word	4.8

Readability
Passive Sentences	2%
Flesch Reading Ease	51.3
Flesch-Kincaid Grade Level	10.9

OK

And, just for fun, here's the readability statistics for the 104-word sentence in the previous case study.

Readability Statistics ? ✕

Counts
Words	104
Characters	573
Paragraphs	1
Sentences	1

Averages
Sentences per Paragraph	1.0
Words per Sentence	104.0
Characters per Word	5.4

Readability
Passive Sentences	0%
Flesch Reading Ease	0.0
Flesch-Kincaid Grade Level	47.3

OK

The Readability Index is very useful as a benchmark, because it can give you a good indication of areas you need to work on—you might tend to write long sentences, or use a lot of passive voice. However, you shouldn't rely too heavily on it, because, as mentioned above, the only thing it measures is word length and sentence length. You need to make sure your writing is also properly planned and structured, and appropriate for your audience, which means using your judgement. If, for example, you're writing for a specialist website, your grade level can be higher and your reading ease lower than if you're writing for schoolchildren.

9.2. Writing for the web

Writing for the web is quite a different style to writing for print, although the principles of Plain English (as outlined in Chapter 9.1) still apply. Before you begin writing your content, you should identify your content's audience and purpose, and start thinking about the way you're going to structure your content and make it accessible to disabled users. See Chapter 5.3 for details on how to do this.

Once you've worked out who you're writing for and why, it's time to think about the nuts and bolts of your content.

Structure and style

As discussed in Chapter 5.3, web readers scan pages, rather than reading every word. This means you need to structure your content to improve scannability, and write in a style that is engaging and easily understood. There are a few ways of doing this:

- **Use headings and subheadings.** Most writers don't use nearly enough headings. On the web, these are the things your reader will jump to, so make sure they're informative.

- **Include a short summary** (one to two sentences) under the main heading so that your reader knows what the article is about.

- **Break your content into chunks**, rather than one big paragraph. Each paragraph should only discuss a single topic.

- **Keep your sentences and your paragraphs short.** See Chapter 9.1 for tips on how to do this.

- **Use the 'inverted pyramid' structure** (as outlined in Chapter 6.3), which means starting with the most important information. Ideally, you should be able to delete the bottom two-thirds of your article without affecting the most important information at the top.

- **Use bulleted/numbered/alphabetised lists**—these draw the eye and are easy for the reader to digest.

- **Include hyperlinks** to other relevant information on your site or other sites.

- **Use relevant images or graphics** to enhance your text, but make sure you make them accessible (see Chapter 5.3 for more information on accessibility).

- **Include a call to action** (e.g. 'buy now' or 'subscribe to our newsletter').

- **Use one-sentence paragraphs** to create a sense of urgency and make the content punchier.

- **Make your writing personable**—use 'I', 'we', 'us', 'you'.

- **Use examples, anecdotes and analogies**—these personalise and humanise your writing.

- **Think about your audience's level of education and use words they're comfortable with.** Avoid complex words, jargon and acronyms. Write to inform, not impress.

- **Make your writing style relaxed and informal** (although still appropriate for your organisation). Even for formal organisations, the website content needs to be less formal than in other publications.

- **Be direct, to the point and say exactly what you mean.** Avoid fluffy introductions.

- **Use verbs not nouns** (e.g. 'please consider this' rather than 'this is for your consideration').

- **Make your content interesting**—use an attention-grabbing headline and don't be afraid to be a bit quirky. Use topical content. Tell stories. Present it in an interesting way, e.g. infographics.

- **Don't oversell your product/service/organisation** or push the user into engaging with it.

- **Make sure your voice fits with the personality of your brand** (see Chapter 9.1). Both words and visual design will impact your voice. Choices about tense, conjunctions, active or passive voice will also affect the voice. Generally write in present tense and active voice.

Relevance and usefulness

Your content needs to meet the needs and goals of the personas you created in your planning stage (see Chapter 5.3). In short, it needs to be relevant to your audience.

Your content should be either useful or entertaining—preferably both, but never neither. It can help to look at what your competitors are doing, and whether their content is more useful to your users than yours. Do some more research and understand exactly what users want to get out of your content.

Give your users practical advice—checklists work well, which is why we're seeing a proliferation of '9 ways to do X' articles. They've even been given their own term: 'listicles' (a portmanteau of 'list' and 'article'). Think about how you can phrase your content to give the user instructions or tips.

Accuracy and credibility

In order to build trust in your website and brand it's essential that your content is accurate and credible. Ask yourself if your content is believable. Can it be trusted? Is it well-written (no typos)?

You need to have the expertise to write about the topic. If you're not an expert, you need to check your content with an expert. Research the topic. Check your facts from multiple sources. If it's incorrect you'll lose credibility.

Currency and consistency

Your content needs to be up to date (see Chapter 5.3 for more on reviewing and maintaining your content). Informational content can be reviewed every three to six months. Other content has a shorter shelf-life. Lists of events date immediately after the event is over and make it obvious that the website isn't maintained properly. News also ages quite quickly, particularly if it contains dates. If it's not current it needs to be taken off the front page and archived. Timetables also need to be reviewed as regularly as possible, as they contain lots of small pieces of information that can date. Currency doesn't necessarily mean it has to be new, just that it has to be regularly reviewed. If you've reviewed your content and it's still up to date and relevant, then you don't necessarily need to change it, but out-of-date content will negatively affect your organisation's reputation and will come across as unprofessional.

The content on various pages and on your social media accounts needs to be consistent. This is particularly important if more than one person is creating content for the website. You need to have a consistent voice in your writing, and stylistic written elements such as the use of abbreviations also need to be standardised. Inconsistency will make the site or account feel disjointed.

Findability

There's no point creating content if it can't be found. People find content through search engines, by linking from other websites, and through menus (navigation), internal links and internal search functions on your website. Good navigation can help people find content easily by laying it out in menus that are logical and easy to use. Labels need to explain clearly what they're about, and need to match the content. Internal links need to be understandable and their labels, as with labels in the menus, must also match the content. Internal search engines need to give the users the content they're looking for.

Include keywords in your content, especially in headings and the page title, to ensure your content will be displayed near the top of a search engine results page. Use analytics to check if people are linking to your site from other websites, and look at how your content is being received on social media. People will share content they find useful and relevant.

Scannability

Keywords help the user scan the page and find what they're looking for. Including keywords will make your user more interested and will also help with search engine optimisation. Your personas (see Chapter 5.3 for details on developing personas) can give you an indication of what those keywords are. If you're not getting this from your personas, you need to do a bit more user research—talk to your audience and find out what they want and the kind of words they use (e.g. for sport, they may use 'game' or 'tournament' as well as 'match'). Look at your competitors' sites and see what keywords they use. Analytics can also tell you what keywords people are putting into search engines.

Keywords need to be in headings and sometimes also subheadings. They also need to be in the content and links, because both users and search engines scan the page and look at headings, links and lists.

Using headings and subheadings also makes the content much easier to scan. Headings need to be short, concise, simple, and factual. They should be fragments rather than full sentences, and should be written in sentence case, not all-caps. Your headings should contain keywords, and should not contain acronyms or abbreviations (unless they've become brand names, like 'Qantas').

Your main heading (tagged as <h1> in HTML) will show up in your search results. The title of your page (which appears in the browser tab, rather than on the page itself, tagged as <title> in HTML) will also appear in the search results. You'll generally have a limit of about 70 characters for the title.

Links

When you're inserting links, don't include the words 'click here,' 'here' or 'more'. This doesn't tell the user where they're going or entice them to go there, and it isn't considered good practice. Instead, use the keywords you've identified in your links and make them action-oriented. You don't need to write a URL out in full—just put your link on a keyword, as users will automatically click on keywords. If your link is on the wrong word (not the keyword) they'll become confused.

Another good reason to put links on keywords is accessibility. Screen readers will scan the page and tell the user what the links are, but if they all say 'more' the user won't be confident about which one to follow. See Chapter 5.3 for more on accessibility.

Similarly, don't put two links right next to each other, because it will confuse the user and they'll either click the wrong one or miss them altogether. Don't have too many links on a page—you want enough to be useful, but don't overdo it. They should be long enough to be clickable (e.g. more than one word).

Links can be highlighted with a different colour but no longer need to be underlined. However, because many people still associate underlining with links, don't use underlining to emphasise areas of your text (use bold or italics instead).

If you want your users to be able to contact you, rather than showing email addresses in full—which is clunky and makes you vulnerable to spam—put a 'contact us' link in. Rather than linking this to an email address, which will open an email client, link it to a contact form, because you can't be sure that all users will have their email clients configured correctly. Providing a form will ensure they'll be able to contact you even if their email client isn't working.

If you're including a download link, tell the user what it is they're downloading (e.g. a brochure, a form), the file type (e.g. a PDF) and how big it is (because people with unreliable internet or limited download capacity may decide not to download it at that time). As with links to webpages, include the download link on the keywords, rather than saying 'more'.

Visual and audio content

Well-chosen images or video can break up your written content, communicate information in a way that's different and more memorable, and give greater insight into what you're discussing. Some examples of visual content include:

- Screenshots—these are especially useful if you're showing how to do something in a computer program or app

- Infographics—these are information represented in a graphical way, and may mix charts, illustration, images and written content

- Maps

- Diagrams

- Charts

- Tables—these need to be big enough to be legible

- Videos—videos need captioning and transcripts, and rely on the user being in an environment where they can play them, so you also need to provide some written supporting content in case they can't

- Pull-out quotes—these split up the page, making it more scannable, interesting and eye-catching.

Forms

Particularly if you have a mailing list, you may need to develop a sign-up form to appear on your website. Mailing list providers like MailChimp provide sign-up form templates that you can adapt to your needs.

Sign-up forms need an informative heading, and they may also have some short introductory copy explaining what they're for, although this isn't essential. Your form will also have labels and form fields, detailing what information the user needs to include and whether it's mandatory. It may also have drop-downs and radio buttons, and there should also be a call-to-action button—'sign up' or 'submit'—that encourages the user to do something with it. You may also need to include a privacy policy at the bottom of the form.

Consider what type of information you need from the user and what you need to tell them. Try to ask for less information rather than more (e.g. do you really need their name or just their email address?). People are more likely to sign up if the process is quick and not intrusive.

You also need to think about the messages that will be triggered when a user fills out a form. There is a scale of messages from positive to negative:

- Success messages—'thank you for your order', 'your form has been submitted' etc.

- Information messages—scheduled website maintenance

- Warning messages—'you will be logged out in one minute' (this is a bit more severe than an information message; it gives the user a sense of urgency and encourages them to take action)

- Error messages—'the email address or password you entered is incorrect' (prevents the user from moving forward unless they fix the error)

The tone of voice in messages is important—it needs to match that of your overall brand. The message tone doesn't necessarily have to be formal if your overall brand voice is casual or cheeky. However, it's important that you (or another content writer) rather than the website developer writes the message, because otherwise you'll potentially end up with abrupt, uninformative messages like 'server error'.

Writing your content

This checklist is designed to help you plan and write your content. For tips on language and grammar, see Chapter 9.1 and Appendix D.

- **Define the page topic.** There should be one topic per page. If you want to talk about multiple things, split them into multiple pages.

- **Define the page purpose.** Is it to inform, engage or entertain?

- **Define your users' needs and goals.** You've probably already done this for the whole website, but think about it for this page specifically. What are they wanting to get out of it?

- **Define your keywords.** Make a list to refer back to when writing your content.

- **Work out where the user should go next.** Decide exactly what you want the user to do with the information you give them, e.g. print something off, go to a page within your website, or go to another website.

- **Think of a heading.** Write it first then go back and tweak it after you've written the content.

- **Make a list of some of the content you want to get across to the user.** This will give you an understanding of where pieces of content will be on the page.

- **Think of images, video and audio that you can use to enhance your content.** Think about what you're going to include before you start, because this will affect the way you write your content.

Always review and edit your content before publishing it. See Chapter 9.4 for more detail on how to edit your work. As your web content should be written in Plain English, revise your work in line with the principles set out in Chapter 9.1.

CASE STUDY

INTEGRATING YOUR CONTENT

Love Makes A Way is an Australian Christian refugee advocacy organisation known for conducting peaceful civil disobedience actions, such as prayer vigils in the offices of government ministers, in order to protest the treatment of refugees in Australia's offshore detention centres. Below is a screenshot of its desktop homepage (note, at full size each horizontal panel takes up the width and height of the monitor, and the menu bar stays visible even as the user scrolls down the page).

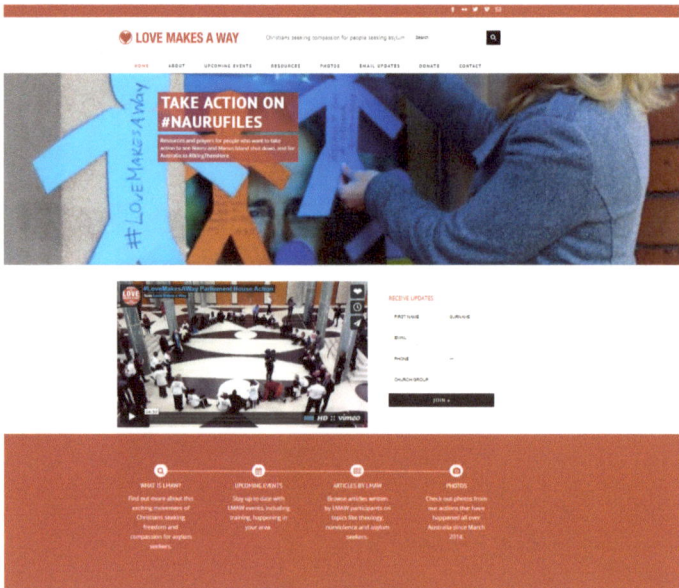

As you can see, most of the content on the front page is very visual—it has large photos (the main photo rotates through several images), a video of the group's recent sit-in at

Parliament House, and a sign-up form for its mailing list. Its mission statement is succinct and prominently placed next to the site's main heading. The menus and labels are clear and there is an internal search function prominently displayed. The user can also scroll down for more information, including endorsements from prominent figures (not displayed here) and a Twitter feed.

Other pages on the site are more text-heavy, but also include prominent photos and multimedia, including links to social media. The tone of the content is informal but passionate, reflecting the group's origins as a grassroots movement started by young people. The organisation's Christian values are prominently displayed, but the content also focuses on broader appeal by focusing on themes such as shared humanity.

9.3. Writing for social media

Social media has brought with it its own unique writing style. What works in a physical brochure or on a website will often sound too formal or stilted on social media. You need to remember that social media is first and foremost about relationship-building; you may want to use it as part of your marketing to sell tickets or get people onto your email list, but unless you have a good relationship with your followers you won't meet your goals.

With that in mind, here are some tips for writing effective social media posts. These apply to most networks, although you will need to tweak them slightly depending on the platform. LinkedIn, for example, has a more formal voice than Facebook, while Twitter is constrained by having to keep your posts to less than 140 characters.

- **Keep it casual.** Pretend you're writing for a friend, not your boss.

- **Use personal pronouns.** 'I', 'we', 'us' and 'you' all make the reader feel included.

- **Keep it short.** People's attention spans are shrinking.

- **Use lots of white space.** On platforms with no length constraints, like Facebook, you want to avoid big chunks of text.

- **Keep the important information up the top.** Some platforms hide the bottom parts of long posts behind a 'read more' tag, which most people won't click.

- **Use action-oriented language.** You want your reader to do something, so ask a question or encourage them to take action in some way.

- **Check before you post.** Remember your audience and think laterally to make sure your post can't be misinterpreted.

- **Share something useful.** Don't just promote your brand—your post needs to be either informative or entertaining, or ideally both.

- **If you're linking to an article, make sure you have a great headline.** You want to draw the reader in and make them keep reading.

CASE STUDY

THE PERSONAL TOUCH

Even if your organisation's overall brand voice is more formal, you still need to be quite casual on social media or you put too much distance between yourself and your followers. This can sometimes mean injecting a bit of humour or something that gives your organisation a 'personal touch' (although anything vulgar or offensive should be avoided). A number of police and emergency services organisations do this very well, especially on Facebook and Twitter. The Australian Federal

---

Police (AFP) account on both these networks is a particularly good example. Here's an AFP Facebook post about how to take a safe selfie, which went viral.

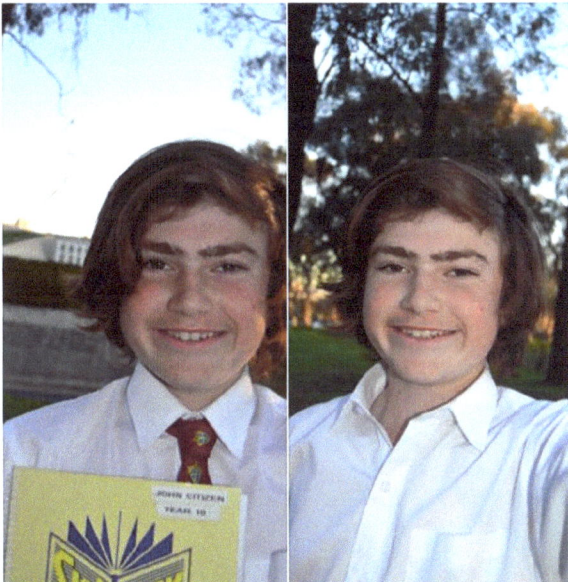

Australian Federal Police added 2 new photos
16 August at 14.41

What's in a selfie? Spot the difference between the following two photos for some hints.

The photo on the left tells us who the boy is, roughly how old he is, where he goes to school, and possibly even where he lives.

ThinkUKnow how to stay safe online? Please be wary of what you, and your kids, are posting online.

For more information on how to stay safe, or to book a free cyber safety presentation, go to ThinkUKnow Australia.

The voice in the post is casual, but this doesn't diminish the seriousness of the public safety message. The paragraphs are short and written in Plain English, and the image is eye-catching and reinforces the main point. The post uses action-oriented language ("spot the difference") and ends with a call to action ("book a free cyber safety presentation") and a link to more information.

Images and multimedia

Including images and videos in your social media posts will boost your followers' interactions with them, whether that's likes, shares or comments. There are a few things you need to think about when adding videos to your social media posts, which are detailed in Chapter 4.6, including length, sound and autoplay. You also need to keep accessibility in mind and make sure your content doesn't rely solely on the image. In the AFP post above, for example, the text includes a description of the differences between the two images, which would allow someone with a screen reader to still understand the main message. For more on accessibility, see Chapter 5.3 and Chapter 9.2.

If your organisation creates a lot of visual content, Instagram is a particularly good platform. Because Instagram is an image-sharing platform, your photos need to be able to carry the post essentially by themselves (meaning they need to be higher-quality in terms of composition and interest than, for example, on Facebook). You can add text, hashtags and mentions to Instagram posts, but don't rely too heavily on the text (although you should use hashtags for best effect).

Hashtags and mentions

Hashtags and mentions are primarily used on Twitter and Instagram, although you sometimes also see hashtags on Facebook. A hashtag (#topic) is used to aggregate information by topic. A mention (@username) is used to interact with specific people. Both can be used either in the main body of the post or appended after the main text.

You can either interact with existing hashtags or create your own. If you choose to engage with an existing hashtag, make sure you understand what it's about. For example, the hashtag #yesallwomen deals with women's experiences of sexual harassment and assault. It would therefore be completely inappropriate to use it outside of this context, e.g. "#yesallwomen are guaranteed to love our new play, 'Motherhood', on until 25 September!". That said, you're generally going to get more traction for your post if you engage with existing hashtags rather than creating your own, as it's very hard to get reach for a new hashtag unless it's supported by an extensive marketing campaign.

In addition, if you create your own hashtag, remember that once it's out there you lose control over it. For this reason you need to think very carefully about whether it can be misinterpreted or hijacked. A lot of this depends on knowing your audience. For example, in November 2015 the Victorian Taxi Association, which represents taxi drivers in the Australian state of Victoria, decided to fight back against the arrival of Uber with an extensive social media marketing campaign built around the Twitter hashtag #YourTaxis. They asked Twitter users to "tell us your taxi stories," clearly hoping for some positive reinforcement. What they got were 140-character diatribes about cab drivers who refused short fares, drove dangerously, had poor hygiene, sexually or verbally harassed passengers, or couldn't find major landmarks. This was a social media blunder that should have been foreseeable, given the industry's poor reputation, and clearly resulted from misunderstandings about their audience and how widespread poor public opinion of the brand really was.

If you've got a story that resonates with the public—particularly a human interest one about adversity—a hashtag campaign can be very effective. However, before you start one, make sure you've got a strategy in place for responding to questions, complaints and trolls.

9.4. Editing and proofreading

There is a common misconception that editing is all about finding and fixing spelling mistakes or typos. In fact, an editor's job is much broader.

Much like an inverted pyramid, editing should start wide and gradually narrow in focus. This means starting with structural and copy-editing before moving on to proofreading. In some situations, such as book publishing, substantive editing, copy-editing and proofreading are done by separate people. In other contexts, a professional editor may combine them (such as a mix of structural and copy-editing).

Appendix D contains an editing checklist, which can be used to guide you through the editing process. There are also numerous editing resources available online.

Substantive/structural editing

A structural edit focuses on the document as a whole. It examines the document's structure, logic and flow, and takes into account the intended audience and the document's overall purpose. This may involve suggesting substantial changes to the work. Structural edits do not focus on language.

Copy-editing

As well as correcting any linguistic or grammar mistakes, a copy-editor will ensure a document conforms to house style with regard to language, voice, register, spelling and grammar, and may also check tables, illustrations, captions, references and tables of contents, depending on the scope of their brief. This process may also involve fact-checking, formatting, and deleting or modifying inconsistencies or repetition.

Proofreading

Proofreading is the final step in the pre-publication process. It is usually done when the text returns from the designer (if applicable) and is in its final, fully formatted form. This is the final check for any errors in spelling, grammar and punctuation, as well as oddly breaking lines or words (known as 'widows' and 'orphans').

When to hire a professional

If you have a document that needs to be produced to a professional standard, such as an annual report or a book, it's worth employing a professional editor. Although professional editing can be expensive, depending on the length of the publication and the depth of the edit—because most editors work to an hourly rate, and long publications and in-depth edits take more time—it's an investment that will ensure your document is at the best standard it can be.

Editors can be engaged for a variety of tasks, and a light edit or proofread of a short document will not be prohibitively expensive. Many editors work freelance and you can find them through your country's Society of Editors (or equivalent), many of which also have state/provincial branches. Many editors specialise in particular areas, such as fiction or non-fiction, so make sure you engage one who meets your needs. For a handy decision-making flowchart on when to employ a professional, see Afterword: When Should I Hire a Professional?

Even if you choose not to use a professional editor, it's important to edit and proofread all your organisation's documents before they're released. Ideally, you should have enough time built into your deadline for the document to 'rest' between the writing and editing phases, so that you're not too familiar with it when it comes time to edit it. Alternatively, ask someone unfamiliar with the document to edit it for you. This person should ideally have high-level writing skills and be able to analyse information critically.

9.5. Developing a style guide

Many organisations, especially those involved in the media or publishing industries, have a 'house style'—a way of writing that is particular to that organisation and is set out in their style guide. The style guide's purpose is not to determine what is 'correct' and 'incorrect', but rather to serve as a reference point if there is any confusion and to ensure consistency across the organisation's brand. Your style guide will lay out how to articulate the brand voice you decided was appropriate for your audience during your strategic planning.

There are two types of style guides. Visual style guides are aids for designers and contain things like your brand's colours, font, logos and templates. Content style guides contain details of your organisation's preferred spelling, terminology, voice, and word usage. Style guides can range in length from a few pages to an entire book; for example, the Australian Government's *Style manual for authors, editors and printers*, which is the basis for all Australian government writing, is over 500 pages long and is extremely comprehensive.

As well as providing consistency across your organisation, style guides are also useful if you're working with a freelance editor. Providing your editor with a style guide will speed up the process and ensure their edits are consistent with your brand.

Your style guide is a living document, so it should be updated regularly to take new usages into account. It should be easily accessible within your organisation, whether it's produced in hard copy, published on your website or stored in a shared drive.

Visual style guide

Visual style guides set out all the elements related to your brand's appearance, presentation and design. This allows you to ensure consistency across all your publicity material, whether physical or online, even if you're working with different designers. Your visual style guide may include:

- Logo size and placement (and how not to use the logo)
- Colour palette (including hex codes/RGB for web use and CMYK/Pantone for printing)
- Fonts (for headings and body text)
- Any iconography or patterns that your organisation uses in its design
- Photography style (including examples for reference)
- Graphics style (including examples for reference)
- Web-specific elements (such as navigation buttons or error pages)
- Content templates.

Creating a visual style guide is a specialised skill, so it's best to work with a graphic designer on this. Your designer can prepare a style guide as part of working with you on your overall branding, including designing your logo. If your organisation is likely to produce a lot of publicity material, a visual style guide is vital to ensuring brand consistency. The quickest way to appear unprofessional is to have a variety of fonts, colours and styles across your brand.

Content style guide

Style guides for written content contain details of the way your organisation expects its content to be written. These may include:

- The version of English spelling that your organisation uses (e.g. American, British, Australian, Canadian)

- Which dictionary/thesaurus should be used to check spelling or usage (e.g. Merriam-Webster, Oxford, Macquarie)

- Preferred spelling of words commonly used by your organisation (e.g. Asia-Pacific not Asia Pacific)

- Use of inclusive language

- Any specific points of grammar, such as active voice

- Specialised punctuation, including the use of bullet points or numbered lists, and the organisation's preferred use of hyphens, en-dashes and em-dashes (but not punctuation that should be commonly understood, like the correct use of apostrophes)

- Formatting

- Accepted acronyms and abbreviations (which ones are acceptable without spelling them out in full)

- Terminology (how organisation-specific terminology should be explained)

- Words that should be avoided

- Capital letters (especially if there are organisation-specific proper nouns)

- Headings

- Numbers and measurement

- Tone and register (casual, informal, formal)

- Brand voice

- Reading level

- Phrases

- Methods of citation

- Any stylistic devices unique to the organisation.

Style guides can be structured in different ways, but the main thing is that they have to be easy to navigate. They're not designed to be read cover-to-cover; rather, your writers will use them as a resource that they dip in and out of. For this reason, they need to have a clear table of contents and ideally an index as well. If you're publishing it online, the contents page should be hyperlinked to the relevant sections.

The other important thing to note is that you don't have to develop a guide completely from scratch. There are a number of comprehensive commercial style guides, such as *The Chicago Manual of Style* (which is over 1000 pages long) that you can use as the basis for your organisation's style guide. Think of the contents of your style guide as being in addition to the comprehensive guide, rather than repeating things from it. For example, most Australian government departments have their own departmental style guides based on the official government *Style manual for authors, editors and printers*. The convention is to first consult the departmental guide and, if it doesn't contain specific guidance, to then consult the *Style manual*. This way, you're prioritising your brand-specific style, but can still give your writers general guidance through the use of a commercial style manual. Many of these manuals, such as *Chicago*, now also have extensive online support. Developing your style guide this way will also allow you to keep it short (ideally no more than five pages), meaning that it is more likely to be used.

When developing your style guide, make sure you consult the people who will actually be using it—your writers and editors. They'll be able to tell you if there are different usages in the organisation and help you select the most appropriate. Have a plan in place to regularly review and update the style guide, and a method for keeping track of possible changes in the interim. Your style guide is a living document and will need to adapt to evolving language, such as words going in and out of fashion or changing in meaning. This is especially true in organisations that deal with technology or media, where language changes fast.

OVERVIEW

You should try to write all your communications—especially online—in Plain English. Plain English emphasises writing clearly and concisely using commonly understood terms, in a style that is appropriate for your audience and easy for them to understand.

Euphemisms, jargon, acronyms, technical terms, clichés and words that aren't commonly understood should all be avoided in Plain English writing.

Writing in active voice is one of the best ways to get your point across clearly, and it's particularly essential in web writing or anything intended for the general public.

Other elements to consider in your writing include sentence length, cohesion, word choice, voice, register and tone.

The Microsoft Word Readability Index is useful for indicating flaws in your writing that may affect its readability. Readability is a measure of how easy it is for your reader to understand your writing straight away.

Web content needs to be structured to improve scannability, and written in a style that is engaging and easily understood. Things to consider include relevance, usefulness, currency, consistency, findability, scannability, and the use of multimedia.

Social media posts are generally more casual than other forms of writing. Even if your organisation's overall brand voice is more formal, you still need to be quite casual on social media or you put too much distance between yourself and your followers. This can sometimes mean injecting a bit of humour or something that gives your organisation a 'personal touch'.

Including images and videos in your social media posts will boost your followers' interactions with them.

Hashtags can be a great way of tapping into a particular topic or community, but if you choose to engage with an existing hashtag make sure you understand what it's about. If you create your own hashtag, think very carefully about whether it can be misinterpreted or hijacked.

If you have a document that needs to be produced to a professional standard, such as an annual report or a book, it's worth employing a professional editor. Even if you choose not to use a professional editor, it's important to edit and proofread all your organisation's documents before they're released. Professional editing can involve structural or copy-editing, proofreading, or a combination.

Visual and content style guides serve as a reference point if there is any confusion, and ensure consistency across your organisation's brand. Your style guide should lay out how to articulate the brand voice you decided was appropriate for your audience during your strategic planning.

Chapter 10

Other Tools

One of the exciting things about growth of digital communications over the last few years is the proliferation of tools that previously were out of reach of individuals or small organisations. This chapter gives an overview of some useful free or low-cost tools, from surveys and petitions to crowdfunding, apps and cloud storage. It also covers some popular freelancer sites and provides some tips on working with freelancers.

10.1. Surveys

Community organisations can use surveys in a variety of ways. They're useful for market research—what do your customers want and need?—or to check the satisfaction of your members and your wider audience.

SurveyMonkey is the most popular online tool for building and distributing surveys. The basic package is free (up to 10 questions and 100 responses per survey), but you can upgrade to access more sophisticated analytics and other tools.

You can design your survey to match your branding (although some features, like including a logo, require an upgraded plan) and build it either from scratch or based on templates relevant to your industry. SurveyMonkey also provides tips and training on how to build surveys, collect results and analyse data, and a wide range of analytics that lets you go into quite a bit of statistical depth if desired.

10.2. Useful apps

These days, there's an app available for just about any task you can think of (and probably a fair few you can't). If you're after something specific, the best way is to do a generic web search (e.g. 'productivity apps'), but here are just a few that may come in handy for your organisation.

Filmic Pro

Filmic Pro is an incredibly powerful app that turns your smartphone into a full high-definition video camera. Available for both iOS and Android for around $10, it gives you control over all the settings in your phone's camera that you need to shoot professional-quality video, such as aperture, shutter speed, ISO, white balance, resolution, frame rate and audio. Although it's a steep learning curve initially—and it will help if you already have some understanding of the principles of videography—it's a cheap and compact alternative to a professional-quality camera. Filmic Pro's website also sells a range of video and audio gear designed specifically for smartphones, such as lenses, stabilisers, microphones, cases, sliders and lights, if you want to take your videography to the next level. There is also a companion app, called Filmic Remote, which lets you control Filmic Pro wirelessly from a second device.

Ripl

Ripl is a fun little app that lets you create animated posts for social media. You choose a photo, add text, choose a fancy template and customise the fonts and colours, add a caption and hashtags, then post directly to the social network of your choice (Instagram or Facebook work best; on Twitter it posts a link rather than the video). The basic package is free, but features like adding your own logo or music and scheduling posts are restricted to the paid version.

Skype

Skype was one of the first commercial voice-over-internet-protocol (VoIP) applications that provided free video chat and voice calls using data rather than phone networks, and it grew so ubiquitous that it's now become a verb. Newer products, such as Apple's FaceTime, or social media apps like WhatsApp and WeChat, have now caught up to or even superseded Skype, but its large market share still makes it many people's preferred choice for video calls, as it's likely their contacts will have a Skype account but may not have access to other services.

Slack

Slack is the current darling of team communications tools. A web-based instant messaging tool with its own app for iOS and Android (which syncs automatically with anything done on the desktop version), Slack lets you create your own team of users. Only people in that team can see your conversations, and within the team you can create different 'channels' for different topics, at varying levels of privacy—open, for things like projects; private, for sensitive topics; and direct messaging for one-on-one communications. You can also share files, and it's compatible with cloud storage services like Dropbox and Google Drive. Everything is also saved into a searchable archive, making it a great alternative to group emails. The basic plan is free for teams of all sizes.

Asana and Trello

Asana and Trello are project-management tools that, like Slack, have both desktop and app versions. These types of tools let you allocate tasks in your project to different people in your team and track your deadlines and workflow. They also contain instant messaging tools, a calendar to track your work, and file sharing. Asana is integrated with Dropbox, Google Drive and Slack. Trello's basic version is integrated with Dropbox and Google Drive, and its paid version integrates with a range of other services, including MailChimp. Both have free plans, although their more sophisticated features are restricted to paid plans. These types of tools would suit volunteer organisations or committees that have lots of projects on the go, especially if they're assigned to different people.

10.3. Online petitions

Gone are the days when putting together a petition meant traipsing door-to-door collecting signatures. Now, anyone can start a petition with a few clicks and forward it through social media. There are a number of online petition sites, but Change.org is the largest and best-known.

Change.org is a non-profit organisation that hosts online petitions for free. It bills itself as a social enterprise that aims to promote social change by giving ordinary people a platform through which to reach decision-makers.

The growth in online petition sites has coincided with a change in the media landscape that means journalists now source a lot of their stories through social media. Consequently, petitions that go viral on social media are likely to get picked up by traditional media and given greater exposure.

However, because there are now so many petitions out there on issues big and small, it can be hard to make yours stand out. Your choice of issue will be part of it—something that resonates with large numbers of people is naturally going to go further than something that is only important to a select few. However, although sheer numbers are important, it's also important to consider who is signing. For example, you're petitioning your local council about an issue important to your local community. You may have relatively few signatures because the issue is so localised, but if half of those signatures are from major community and business leaders, your petition will carry more weight.

As with all your other communications, your petition needs to be targeted and run in a professional manner. This means:

- Tell your story professionally and succinctly, and make sure there are no spelling or grammatical errors. Emotion can sometimes be a useful narrative tool, but decision-makers are more likely to be swayed by logic. Don't just highlight the problem—put forward a solution too.

- Target your decision-makers carefully. There's no point sending a petition to someone who has no power to do anything about your issue.

- Target your supporters. It's good to get a large number of supporters if possible, but think also about targeting high-profile people who have an interest in your issue, as having some high-profile names will help add weight to your petition.

- Deal professionally with your supporters. Keep them updated on any developments and let them know when you've reached a resolution. Also consider giving them information about other ways they can get involved.

- Don't feed the trolls. If you put forward a strong opinion, you're likely to hear from people who oppose it equally strongly. Make sure you deal with any negative comments in a calm and professional way. Try to encourage conversations between people of differing views.

10.4. Crowdfunding

'Crowdfunding' refers to raising money from a large number of people to fund a project, small business, charity drive or other enterprise. The most common way to do this is through an online crowdfunding site. There are a substantial number of crowdfunding sites around, and many focus on specific types of projects or industries.

Regardless of their targeted industry, crowdfunding sites tend to work in similar ways. A person seeking funding proposes a project, a funding goal and a timeframe. Supporters pledge to make a certain contribution, often for a small reward (the rewards increase in value the higher the pledge). If the funding goal is reached in the timeframe, the project is fully funded and supporters are contacted to contribute their money. If the goal isn't reached, the project is not funded and no money is collected (an 'all-or-nothing' model). However, on some sites—particularly charity-focused ones—the proposer gets to keep whatever money is pledged, even if it falls short of the target (a 'keep-what-you-get' model).

A few of the major crowdfunding sites are detailed below. Some of these are for-profit sites, meaning they charge a commission and/or set-up fees, while others are non-profit. Do your research and make sure you choose a platform that suits your needs.

Kickstarter

Kickstarter is a crowdfunding platform for the creative industries—it focuses on helping artists, designers, musicians, filmmakers and other creatives fund their work. It uses an all-or-nothing funding model, so if your project fails to meet its target you don't receive any money.

Indiegogo

Indiegogo is open to all projects, from inventions to entrepreneurial start-ups. It is a for-profit enterprise with 5 per cent platform fees and both all-or-nothing and keep-what-you-get funding models.

Pozible

Like Kickstarter, Pozible is focused on the creative industries, but has a wider scope of projects. Its fees vary, from 5 per cent for projects of less than $100,000, to 4 per cent for projects between

$100,000 and $500,000 and 3 per cent for projects over $500,000. Its funding model is all-or-nothing.

Gofundme

Gofundme is a personal crowdfunding website, meaning it focuses on personal causes such as medical expenses, volunteering trips or funerals. Because it is charity-focused, supporters don't get rewards for contributing particular amounts; rather, the premise relies on giving the supporters a feeling of altruism.

Gofundme also has a charity arm, where people can start a fundraising project for a charity from the organisation's list of registered charities (which are all US-based) and then encourage their friends to donate.

Unlike other crowdfunding sites, Gofundme does not set time goals, so the campaign can continue for as long as the organiser wants. Its fee is 5 per cent and its funding model is keep-what-you-get.

Chuffed

Chuffed focuses on non-profit and social enterprise projects. It is a non-profit organisation and its funding model is keep-what-you-get. It does not charge administration fees.

Patreon

Patreon also targets the creative industries, but unlike other crowdfunding models, it aims to provide ongoing rather than one-off funding (based on the traditional idea of patronage for the arts). While the aim of a Kickstarter campaign is to get support for a specific project, Patreon campaigns are about fans funding the creator rather than the project. 'Patrons' provide a tip of a specified amount either monthly or every time the creator releases a new piece of content, and can set a monthly maximum. In return, the artist will offer an exclusive package to their patrons, which may include things like complementary tickets, tutorials or a regular Q&A session.

In principle, crowdfunding sounds like a fantastic way to get a project off the ground, and there is no question that it has given life to projects that otherwise wouldn't have seen the light of day. However, it is also not something to be undertaken lightly, and its success rates are generally low. According to Kickstarter, 305,250 projects have been launched since the site's inception in 2009, of which 107,799 have been successfully funded, giving it a success rate of around 35 per cent.

CASE STUDY

KNOW YOUR POTENTIAL INVESTORS

Just putting a project up on a crowdfunding site will not magically mean that it will suddenly be seen by a host of rich investors. In reality, most of your funding will come from your existing audience or fans. This means that if you don't have much of an audience to begin with, you're unlikely to get a lot of funding. However, even micro-projects can succeed if they have an audience.

For example, a sports-mad young woman in my local community suffered a sporting accident that left her a paraplegic. The local sports clubs that she had been part of banded together to raise money to buy her a sports wheelchair so that she could continue to play. The wheelchair cost several thousand dollars, but they reached their goal, because people in the community knew how life-changing it would be for her and were happy to contribute. They had an audience, and a cause that struck a chord with that audience. But if you're expecting strangers to fund your pet project just because it's something you'd like to do then you'll probably be disappointed.

Before you launch a crowdfunding campaign think carefully about a few things:

- Where will the money will come from? This comes back to having an existing audience.

- How will you drive traffic to your campaign site? You will need a marketing plan for your crowdfunding campaign, which you should incorporate into your overall communications and social media strategies (see Part 1). This includes producing a professional-looking video about your project, as this is the thing that will (hopefully) be shared widely on social media. Don't try to do this on a shoestring.

- What do you offer that's unique? Maybe you already have an established fan base and you're offering them something that they desperately want—your next book/album/artwork/invention. But if you don't, what is it about your project that will draw people in?

- What rewards will you offer your supporters? Be creative here—don't just give them a sample of your eventual product. Think about what will most encourage people to donate. You need to offer them something of value in terms of either a product or an experience.

Crowdfunding can be a great way for cash-strapped volunteer organisations to achieve otherwise unreachable projects. But, like all fundraising and marketing, it needs to be approached strategically, with a good understanding of what you want to achieve and how you plan to do it, or it is likely to fail.

10.5. Cloud storage

Cloud storage—where your documents are stored online in 'the cloud' rather than on your computer's hard drive—has been around for a while now, but many volunteer organisations still aren't taking full advantage of it. As well as being a good way to back up your documents, cloud storage also provides a better way of collaborating on files than emailing them back and forth, especially if your files are large. By keeping a single copy of a file in a shared drive and instituting some practices for tracking edits, you can ensure that everyone on your committee always has access to the most up-to-date version. You can also share links to specific files or folders with people who aren't members of your group, which will enable them to see only that specific document or folder.

Below are some profiles of three of the most popular cloud storage sites, although there are many more available. The main thing is to ensure that everyone in your organisation who needs access is set up with an account to whichever storage service you're using. Accounts on all these sites are free for the basic model, but you'll need to upgrade to a paid plan if you want more storage. Most cloud storage sites also have apps so you can access your files wherever you are.

Dropbox

Dropbox, which started in 2007, is one of the original cloud storage sites. It has 2GB of free storage, although you can earn more by referring people (500MB for every person who signs up, up to 16GB). You can either access your files through the Dropbox site on your web browser or install a version directly to your computer so that it shows up in your file explorer, allowing for easy drag-and-drop.

Google Drive

Two main advantages that Google Drive has over its competitors are, firstly, it's integrated with Google's other products, such as Gmail, Calendar and Docs, so you only need a single account to access them all; and secondly, it provides much more free storage, with 15GB on its free plan.

Google Drive should not be confused with Google Docs, which is a collaboration tool that lets you create web-based text documents, spreadsheets or slides (stored online until you download them) that can be edited by multiple people simultaneously. Google Docs now sits within Google Drive. If you think of it in terms of your computer, Google Docs is like a mashed-up version of Microsoft

Word, Excel and PowerPoint, while Google Drive is like your computer's hard drive, where everything is stored.

OneDrive

OneDrive (previously known as SkyDrive) is Microsoft's cloud storage service. It works with Microsoft Office Online, meaning you can edit documents directly in your browser (much like Google Docs). It provides 5GB of free storage, but it is not as widely used as Dropbox or Google Drive, meaning many people in your organisation may already have accounts for one of those other services rather than for OneDrive.

iCloud

iCloud is Apple's cloud storage service, which it launched in 2011. Although it is an Apple product, there is a Windows version available, although this has to be installed on your PC rather than accessed through a browser. As well as storing your files, iCloud lets you back up your iOS device to it directly (provided you have enough space) and locate lost devices through the Find My iPhone service. iCloud comes with 5GB of free storage. In 2013, Apple launched iWork (a suite of office applications similar to Google Docs—Pages for word processing, Keynote for presentations and Numbers for spreadsheets). It also has iCloud Drive, which is a storage solution similar to Dropbox or Google Drive, although it's not as user-friendly as these two and nowhere near as streamlined for collaboration.

10.6. Freelancer sites

If you decide that you need to hire a professional writer, editor, designer or photographer (see Afterword: When Should I Hire a Professional?) the chances are they'll be a freelancer. They may be working as a sole trader or as a limited liability company, but either way you'll be engaging a small business.

So how do you go about finding a freelance professional?

- **Word of mouth.** Most freelancers get at least some, if not the majority, of their work through word of mouth, so start by asking around. Like tradespeople, a good freelancer will get recommended.

- **Industry bodies.** Industry bodies, such as your local Society of Editors (or equivalent), usually have freelance registers. Going through an industry body will ensure the person you hire has the necessary training and experience.

- **E-work sites.** Many 'e-work' sites have popped up in recent years. Some of these are profiled below, but a word of warning—you get what you pay for. You may find that you can get your work done cheaply through these sites, but this will often come at the cost of quality. If you're not prepared to offer a fair price, you'll find that highly skilled professionals won't respond to your ad. In fact, many established freelancers don't use these sites as they already get enough work through other means. These sites also run on commission, meaning that, unlike hiring a freelancer directly, not all your fee will go to the person who does the work.

Working with freelancers

Before you start working with a freelancer, there are a few things to bear in mind that will help keep the relationship running smoothly.

- **Don't *ever* ask a freelancer to work for 'exposure'.** Would you ask your local restaurant to give you your meal for free in exchange for 'exposure'? No? Then why would you ask it of a creative professional? By doing this you also risk developing a reputation as a time-waster client—established freelancers won't work with you and they'll tell their networks. And apart from anything else, it's just plain exploitative.

- **Freelancers are small businesses.** This means they have to cover the costs of everything usually borne by employers, such as tax and retirement fund payments, out of the fees they charge. So while a quote might seem high to you, remember that anywhere up to 50 per cent of it (depending on the freelancer's financial arrangements) goes straight to the government. It also means that time is money, so don't ask for a face-to-face meeting unless you're prepared to have travel time built into the quote. Go for email, phone or Skype instead.

- **Have a realistic budget.** You get what you pay for, and what you're paying for is the years of experience that established freelancers have behind them. The cost will vary according to the size of your project, the market in your location and the turnaround time, but it's safe to say that $50 or $100 won't cut it unless the job is very small.

- **Know what you want and write it down clearly.** Freelancers of all stripes do their best work when they're properly briefed. The quote you receive should outline the scope of the project, and for anything beyond that you may be charged extra. So knowing what you want will help you avoid 'scope creep' and will save you money.

- **Give them plenty of time.** Rush jobs are always more expensive. Also, many experienced freelancers are booked up weeks or months in advance, so do some planning and enquire early.

- **Make sure you understand and adhere to the terms and conditions.** Many freelancers will have terms and conditions listed that you agree to by accepting a quote. Make sure you understand and adhere to these—especially regarding payment and intellectual property—and if you don't like them, don't accept the quote. Some freelancers may also get you to sign a contract, depending on their business and the size of your project.

- **Pay on time.** This is huge. Many established freelancers ask for full or partial upfront payment, and this is done for a very good reason—many clients don't pay on time and freelancers have to pay their bills in the meantime. You are responsible for your organisation's cash flow, not the freelancer, so if you don't have the money to hire someone, don't. You may be charged late fees if you fail to pay within the terms of the invoice, or in extreme cases you may be referred to a debt collection agency. In addition, many freelancers—especially graphic designers—won't release the final product to you until the final payment has been received, and if you use the product without paying for it under these circumstances you're violating their intellectual property and could leave yourself open to legal action. So make everyone's lives easier and pay on time.

- **Be flexible and easy to work with.** All freelancers get the occasional client from hell, and they usually only work with them once. Don't be that person. This means keeping communication open and recognising that the freelancer will probably need to fit you around other projects, so stick to agreed deadlines and keep your expectations reasonable.

Below are profiles of three of the best-known e-work sites. While these can be a cheaper alternative to hiring an established freelancer directly, remember that you usually get what you pay for. There are also country-specific freelance sites such as The Loop (Australia), so it's worth looking around.

99 Designs

99 Designs is a graphic-design e-work site. Prices are displayed in your local currency. You submit a design brief (for example, for a logo) and choose a price package (ranging from Bronze at A$399, to Platinum at A$1699, where the designers are hand-picked by 99 Designs). After you've submitted your brief and your budget, a range of designers respond with designs and you choose the one you like best. You only pay for the final design. The pros are that this is a fairly quick process, at around a week, and can be useful for smaller projects such as custom illustrations—although in such cases you may actually be able to find a local designer who can do it cheaper. However, if you're after full branding or complex projects you're probably better off working with a local graphic designer with whom you can discuss your needs in more detail.

Upwork

Upwork calls itself a platform for "anything that can be done on a computer"—including copywriting, editing, graphic design and web design, among others. You post a job ad outlining your brief and budget, and freelancers will respond with cover letters, links to their Upwork profiles outlining their experience and a quoted price. You can then interview them and choose the one that best suits your needs. All payments are handled through Upwork, which takes a commission of up to 20 per cent.

Fiverr

Fiverr is an online marketplace where freelancers advertise their skills in a wide range of areas. However, most of these are bargain-basement and of dubious quality. For example, an ad from an 'editor' offers 1000 words edited/proofread in 24 hours for A$6.50, or 10,000 words in 5 days for A$65.50. The market rate for a professional editor in Australia is anywhere between five and ten times that. The main reason these rates are so low is because most of the freelancers advertising on there live in developing countries with much lower costs of living, although some Western freelancers use it for lead generation, offering a cheap starter service that then leads into their full-priced one.

OVERVIEW

Online surveys are useful for market research or to check the satisfaction of your members and your wider audience.

The growth in online petition sites means you can now get your issue in front of decision-makers, the media and the public much more effectively. However, remember that your petition, like your other communications, needs to be targeted and run in a professional manner.

Crowdfunding—raising money from a large number of people to fund a project, small business, charity drive or other enterprise—can be an effective means of fundraising. However, its success rates are generally low and a crowdfunding campaign must be carefully planned.

Cloud storage is a particularly useful tool for volunteer organisations, as it allows easy remote collaboration, version control and file sharing.

Many communications professionals are freelancers and can be found through word of mouth, industry bodies or on e-work sites. However, although e-work sites often offer cheaper rates, you tend to get what you pay for.

Afterword

When Should I Hire a Professional?

Because many volunteer organisations are operating on a shoestring budget, they're often reluctant to spend money on professional design, editing or copywriting. This simplistic calculation, however, often fails to take into account the hidden economics of the decision.

Reputational damage. The longer-term impact on your brand from appearing unprofessional can have flow-on effects that outweigh the cost of employing a professional—such as failing to gain new members, or selling fewer tickets to your performance or event. Nothing turns people off faster than terrible design or sloppy writing. The assumption is that if you don't know what you're doing in these areas (or worse, you don't care), you may not be great at organising the other, more important parts of your group either.

Money is obviously the catch with most volunteer groups, but you need to calculate the outlay against the return. If you're running a fundraiser or a concert and a professionally designed poster will lead to more ticket sales, then it's worth the upfront cost. Similarly, if you're a theatre group producing programs, you'll be able to charge more for something that's well-designed and laid out (as opposed to put together in Microsoft Publisher, or, worse, Word!).

Time and opportunity costs. Unless you have volunteers with specialist skills such as graphic or web design, or editing, it will inevitably take them much longer to produce something of much lower quality than a professional. This is time they could be spending doing other tasks that better serve the organisation and that are a better fit with their skill set. In short, think about time as a resource. Are you spending it in the way that gets you the greatest return on your investment?

To take a personal example: I want to renovate my shed to turn it into an office. I could do it myself, fitting it around my other work, and teach myself the skills I need as I go. But I also don't have the professional tools, so I'll need to buy those too if I want to create something half decent. In summary, it'll take me a lot longer than it would a professional, the quality won't be as good, and I'll have an outlay for tools as well. I'll gain some skills, but I'm never going to be a builder and I really just want the shed done. I make as much or more than a professional builder, so in the end it makes more sense if I do what I'm good at and make money at it, and then pass that money on to the professional builder so they can do what they're good at. Then I get a high-quality result without losing time that's more valuable if I spend it elsewhere, and we're all happy.

With this in mind, here's a simple flowchart to give you some guidance when you're undertaking a project with major design or writing elements.

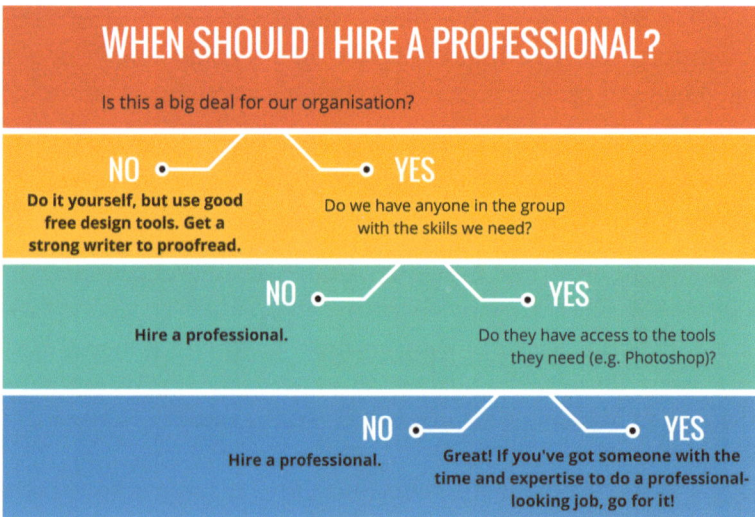

WHEN SHOULD I HIRE A PROFESSIONAL?

Is this a big deal for our organisation?

NO — Do it yourself, but use good free design tools. Get a strong writer to proofread.

YES — Do we have anyone in the group with the skills we need?

NO — Hire a professional.

YES — Do they have access to the tools they need (e.g. Photoshop)?

NO — Hire a professional.

YES — Great! If you've got someone with the time and expertise to do a professional-looking job, go for it!

Is this a big deal for our organisation?

Basically, what is the potential reputational cost of a poor-quality job? Things that fall into this category include:

- Anything that involves your branding (new logo, slogan etc.)

- Major events (e.g. annual fundraising gala, major performance)

- Anything where you're trying to attract new people to your organisation or sell products (e.g. markets/expos that may require banners or other publicity material)

- Any foundational information about your organisation that potential members or supporters are likely to develop a first impression from (website, fliers, programs)

Do we have someone in the group with the skills we need?

Some groups are lucky enough to have people with either formal training in design, photography, writing, editing or related fields, or who are self-taught high-level amateurs. If you have a resource like this, use them! But most importantly, don't take them for granted. Make sure you give them enough lead time and don't have unrealistic expectations. Especially if they're professionals doing it for free, remember that they're donating potentially hundreds or even thousands of dollars' worth of their time to help you. Make sure you credit their work appropriately, and at least give them some chocolate to show your appreciation!

Do they have access to the tools they need?

You can't do decent graphic design in Microsoft Paint—it just doesn't work. So if you've got someone with the skills but they don't have the professional-level tools to do what you want (and you can't provide them), then you need to think about hiring a professional.

Doing it yourself

If you do decide to do it yourself, make it as professional as you can by using all the free and low-cost tools available to you. Graphic design sites like Canva are discussed in Chapter 4.3, and you can now get high-quality printing for banners, fliers etc. done relatively cheaply. Someone with good writing skills will be able to do a basic proofread, although you won't get the same level of detail as with a professional editor.

Above all, remember *you get what you pay for*. Good graphic design, photography, copywriting and editing don't always come cheap, but they can make a huge difference to the success of your brand. Don't just take the cheap option because it's cheap—take the time to do proper calculations on whether you can expect to reap a large enough return from an improved image (and potentially charge higher prices for a professional product) to justify paying a professional.

Appendix A

External Communications Strategy Template

For more details on how to complete this template, please see Chapter 1.

Step 1: Identify your purpose

Why do we want to communicate with people? What are we aiming to achieve?

Step 2: Identify your audience(s)

What are the demographics of the people we are trying to reach?

- Age
- Gender
- Location
- Nationality/ethnicity
- Language
- Interests/hobbies
- Financial status
- Buying habits
- Computer literacy
- Information consumption habits

Step 3: Identify your message(s)

What are we trying to say?

Why should people care?

Why is this newsworthy at this time?

Step 4. Identify your medium(s)

What's the best way to reach our audience(s)?

- How do they like to access information?
- Where do they hang out, both physically and online?

Step 5: Create your content

What's the most engaging way to get our message across?

Step 6: Measure your impact

How many people are we engaging with effectively?

Step 7: Audit your channels

Are there channels we haven't been using that we should be?

Are the channels we're currently using giving us good results?

Appendix B

Internal Communications Strategy Template

For more details on how to complete this template, please see Chapter 2.

Step 1: Identify your organisation's strategic direction

- Where are we currently at?

- Where do we want to be (organisational goals/objectives)?

- How will we achieve these objectives (step-by-step plan)?

- How long will it take?

- How will we know when we've achieved them (measurement)?

Step 2: Identify your purpose

Why do we need to communicate? What are we trying to achieve by this communication? How will this help us meet the organisational goals identified in Step 1?

Step 3: Conduct an audit

What methods are we currently using to communicate with our members? How do our members currently communicate with the leadership team? How do our members stay in touch with each other?

Step 4: Identify your audience(s)

Who do we need to communicate with?

Step 5: Identify your message(s)

What do we want/need to say to our members?

Step 6: Identify your medium(s)

How can we best reach our members? How do they prefer to receive information?

Step 7: Create your content

What's the most engaging way to get our message across?

Step 8: Measure your impact

How many of our members are we engaging with effectively?

Step 9: Develop feedback channels

How can our members best contact us to share their ideas or concerns? Do our members currently feel that they can communicate easily and efficiently with the leadership team? How will we act on information we receive from them? What processes can we put in place to ensure members' information is acted on appropriately?

Step 10: Develop intra-organisation communications

What is the best way for members to communicate with each other? How can we foster a sense of community in our organisation?

Appendix C

Social Media Strategy Template and Content Plan

For more details on how to complete this template, please see Chapter 3.

Step 1: Conduct a social media audit

What's working, what's not, and how can we adjust?

Social network	URL	Follower count	Average weekly activity	Average engagement rate (interactions/reach)

Step 2: Set your goals

How do these contribute to our overall business objectives and other goals as outlined in our external communications plan and/or business plan? Are they SMART (specific, measurable, attainable, realistic and time-bound)?

Step 3: Identify your key message

What do we want the public to know about our organisation? (One line only).

Step 4: Develop your brand voice

How would we like our audience to describe our brand? How can we get these traits into our brand voice?

Once you've decided on your voice, write guidelines for your social media persona and voice and check regularly to make sure your posts are adhering to these.

Step 5: Identify your strategies

Are we using a paid, owned or earned strategy (or some combination of the three)? Identify all your strategies individually so you can track their effectiveness separately.

Consider how you'll support your strategies in terms of the time, people and resources you'll need to allocate.

Step 6: Develop a content plan and calendar

Think about your target audience, goals, brand voice, distribution channels and tactics. Who are we communicating with and how? What do we want to achieve with our content? How will we effectively distribute it to our audience?

Who will create our content? Which channels will we use to distribute it? How often?

What are our key dates for internal and external events that we plan to promote on social media? How much lead time will we need to prepare for these?

In your content calendar:

- Over what period of time will you be developing your content?

- What are the release dates?

- What is the overall duration of your campaign?

- How are you going to support the campaign in terms of staffing and resources?

- Who will be responsible for developing and posting content, monitoring feeds and answering questions?

- Do you have the resources to complete your campaign on time and on budget?

- What reporting intervals will you use to periodically evaluate your campaign (monthly, quarterly, semi-annually)?

Step 7: Allocate roles and responsibilities for maintaining social media accounts

Who will take on the roles of social media director, social media manager and social media coordinator? (In smaller organisations these may all be the responsibility of one person.)

Who will be responsible for creating content? Will there be times of high-volume activity where we need more people active on our accounts? If so, who will these be and how will we train them?

Step 8: Develop a social media policy

Detail the following:

- How your members should use social media

- What kind of use is discouraged

- What process they should follow if they're unsure what's appropriate

- The consequences for social media misuse

Step 9: Develop a critical response plan

Your critical response plan needs to contain the following:

- A social listening protocol for negative sentiment about your brand. Who will be responsible for monitoring this activity and at what point should it be escalated?

- A list of designated decision-makers who are authorised to communicate on your organisation's behalf. What responsibilities do individuals have (e.g. approving messaging, liaising with the media)? What are their contact details (including in an emergency)? If they're unavailable, who will take their place? How will you manage a crisis that drags on for days or weeks?

- A step-by-step action plan for specific situations that would affect your business and the action you'd take to address them.

- Pre-approved messages that can be used in each scenario.

Scenario	Action steps	Pre-approved messages
1.		
2.		
3.		

Step 10: Measure your success

Measure your results against your objectives at regular intervals to determine what works, what doesn't and what you need to adjust.

What are the baselines, targets and benchmarks we will use to report against?

What sort of quantitative measures will we use?

What sort of qualitative measures will we use?

How long are our reporting intervals?

Step 11: Analyse your data and take action

Based on the insights in Step 10, what action do we need to take to optimise our current social media strategies? Do we need to change course altogether?

Do we know what sort of content our community likes best?

What are our competitors doing? Can we borrow successful elements from their strategies?

Appendix D

Editing Checklist

This is a basic editing checklist for double-checking your work before you send or publish it. Not every part will be relevant to every document you create, but most of these are widely applicable.

Structure

- You understand your specific audience(s) and have written with them in mind.

- The key point or argument is unambiguous and easily understood.

- Your document is laid out in either a pyramid (academic writing—introduction, body, conclusion) or inverted pyramid (media or web writing—lead/hook, evidence, conclusion) style. For more detail on this, see Chapter 6.

- In web writing, each of your pages focuses on a single topic.

- Each of your paragraphs focuses on a single idea.

- Each paragraph starts with a topic sentence, then contains supporting details and a concluding or transitional sentence.

- You have used informative headings and subheadings where appropriate.

- Your document flows logically—the paragraphs are in the correct order.

- All your sentences focus on one thought.

- Your sentences vary in length and structure to make the writing interesting.

Writing

- Your tone and register are consistent with your brand voice and appropriate to your audience.

- You have used transitional words where appropriate.

- Your spelling style is consistent throughout the document (American/British/Australian English spelling) and you have consulted the relevant dictionary (American—Merriam-Webster; British—Oxford; Australian—Macquarie).

- Your punctuation style is consistent throughout the document (punctuation rules differ in the American and British systems).

- You have defined all acronyms, abbreviations and technical terms on first use.

- You have deleted all jargon and replaced it with Plain English explanations.

- You have checked for repeated words and used a thesaurus to vary your word choice where necessary.

- You have written mostly in the active voice.

- You have checked for common grammatical errors, including:
  - Wrong word (e.g. affect/effect)
  - Incorrect or missing apostrophes (e.g. 'The dog ate it's bone'; 'Johns bicycle')
  - Unnecessary or missing capitalisation (e.g. 'My daughter lily attends University')
  - Shifts in verb tense (e.g. 'He entered the room where I am watching television')
  - Sentence fragments (e.g. 'The girl sitting on the steps, eating a sandwich')
  - Dangling modifiers (e.g. 'Resembling a house more than a prison, Lisa has found living here has helped her rehabilitation')

- o Unnecessary or missing hyphens (hyphens should only be used with compound adjectives, e.g. 'My log-in name', not phrasal verbs, e.g. 'log in to your account')

- o Quotation marks for emphasis (e.g. 'Buy one, get one "free"!').

Design

- You have engaged a professional designer if necessary

- Your colours, logos and fonts are consistent with your overall brand

- Your text is readable against your background

- Your font is clear and easy to read

- You have applied consistent styles to your headings throughout your document

- You have left enough white space on the page (e.g. by using short paragraphs)

- Your document is correctly formatted

- You have used diagrams and visual aids where necessary

- Your table of contents is up to date

- Your photos and graphics are a high-enough resolution and aren't pixelated

Appendix E

Communications Professionals—Roles

This is a brief introduction to some of the communications professionals that your organisation may seek to hire. Many of these professionals work as freelancers (see Chapter 10.6 for details on how to engage freelancers).

Web designer

Web designers design websites, which means blending technical and aesthetic skills. They aim to create websites that are aesthetically pleasing, appropriate for the target market and technically accessible. This involves analytical skills in terms of designing the structure of the website's information (menus etc.) and also creative skills in making the content—which could be written or visual—clear, easy to find and informative. Most web designers have at least some programming skills and many also have graphic design skills.

Graphic designer

Graphic designers use visual concepts to communicate ideas or information. Graphic design is about much more than just knowing how to use Adobe Photoshop, InDesign or Illustrator; it's about being able to conceptualise information visually and present it in an eye-catching, informative way. Graphic designers also work with clients to develop brand logos or other types of visual identification—many will specialise in particular areas.

Photographer

Photographers obviously specialise in taking photos. However, they are also specialists in digital post-production, and some will also do videography (although this tends to be a separate area of expertise). Photographers will often specialise in particular areas, such as weddings, portraiture, events, theatre or sports photography, so it's important to hire one who covers your field. Including professional-looking photography is one of the easiest ways to improve the overall quality of your promotional material.

Copywriter

Copywriters specialise in writing 'copy' for online and print publications, usually (but not always) in the form of marketing or advertising. They are adept at writing copy that engages the reader and either informs them or persuades them to take a certain action—copywriting is writing with an agenda. Copywriting also involves significant research and editing, and copywriters who write for the web must also be aware of search engine optimisation techniques. For example, a good copywriter would be useful for producing engaging content for a volunteer organisation's website or other promotional materials.

Editor/proofreader

Professional editors usually conduct three major types of editorial work. Substantive or structural editing involves a thorough examination of the structure, logic and flow of the document, while copy-editing involves looking at writing style, voice, register, tone and other technical aspects. Proofreading is the final check for spelling, grammatical and punctuation errors, which usually occurs once the document is in its final layout. For this reason, proofreaders often work closely with graphic designers.

Many editors specialise in either fiction or non-fiction. Some will also undertake formatting tasks, such as applying styles to Microsoft Word documents, or formatting a publication to be produced as an ebook (some designers also specialise in formatting).

Social media manger

Freelance social media managers (also sometimes called community managers) look after an organisation's social media presence. This can include using analytics to monitor the success of marketing strategies, answering queries that come through the organisation's social media pages, producing content, developing and implementing the organisation's social media strategy, and online advertising. Social media managers need to be adept at writing, research, organisation, strategic thinking and specialised computer-related skills like search engine optimisation.

Glossary

Accessible: Employing web design techniques to cater for users with visual, auditory, motor or other impairments.

Add-on: In computing, a utility that enhances a primary program. See 'plugin'.

Algorithm: A self-contained step-by-step set of operations to be performed. Algorithms perform calculation, data processing, and/or automated reasoning tasks.

Alternative text: Text that can be included in a website's HTML code to describe images for visually impaired people.

Analytics: The tools and data available on social networks, email marketing software and websites for measuring your content's reach, targeted demographics and other metrics.

Android: A mobile operating system developed by Google, used in most non-Apple smartphones, tablets and other mobile devices.

App: Short for 'application'—a self-contained piece of software used for a specific purpose, usually downloaded to mobile devices.

Back-end: The aspects of a website that the user doesn't see or interact with (as opposed to front-end, which is the user interface).

Bandwidth: The volume of information per unit of time that an internet connection can handle. Usually expressed in bits per second, e.g. 60 Mbps (megabits per second). The higher the number, the faster the connection.

Base: The number of followers you have on a social media account.

Blog: A regularly updated site written in a conversational style, usually displayed as a series of posts in reverse chronological order.

Bounce rate: How quickly a visitor to a webpage leaves the page or site.

Centralised accountability: A strategy for managing website content where all content must be approved by a central authority (usually a web or communications team/manager) before it goes live. This allows for standardisation and quality control, but can also lead to bottlenecks.

Chunking: The breaking of web content into paragraphs based on topics. This makes it easier for readers to scan quickly.

Click-through rate: The number of people who follow a link from an advertisement or post to your nominated website.

Cloud storage: A method of data storage where data is stored, managed, maintained and backed up remotely and made available to users over a network (typically the Internet).

Colour hex (hexadecimal) code *(web)*: A six-digit, three-byte code used to specify colours for webpages using a hexadecimal format (numbers 0-9 and letters A-F). Each byte (pair of digits) specifies either the red, green or blue values of the colour. Colour hex codes are usually preceded by a # sign (e.g. #E74E36—the orange-red colour used in the diagrams in this book). There are plenty of online converters that allow you to convert between the hex, RGB and CMYK values for a specific colour, which you will need to do if you're using the same colour online and in print.

Content *(web and marketing)*: The textual, visual and aural content that a user experiences on websites—including written material, images, videos and sound clips.

Content calendar/plan: A calendar or table that lays out the content you're going to be communicating, when, how, and who is responsible for it. Content calendars can be used for external communications, internal communications and social media.

Content management system (CMS): A software program or set of applications used to create and manage digital content.

Conversion rate: The number of people who, as a result of your social media strategy, undertake the action you've been encouraging them to do, such as buying a product or signing up to a newsletter.

Cookie *(web)*: A small text file created by a website that is stored in the user's computer either temporarily or permanently, allowing the website to recognise you and keep track of your preferences.

Creative Commons license: A license on creative work (such as photos, music, written material, games or videos) that makes it legally available to others to share or modify for free, as long as the user meets certain conditions.

Crowdfunding: Raising money from a large number of people to fund a project, small business, charity drive or other enterprise, usually by using an online platform.

Crowdsourcing: A portmanteau of 'crowd' and 'outsourcing'—the practice of obtaining services, ideas, feedback or input from a large number of people, usually via the Internet, rather than from traditional sources or suppliers.

CSS: Cascading Style Sheets, a programming language used in conjunction with HTML to define styles on a website, including colour, font, layout, animation and responsiveness.

Curated content: Something you share on social media that you didn't create yourself (i.e. it's curated from another source).

CMYK: A subtractive colour model used in graphic design and printing that describes each colour in terms of the amount of secondary colour (cyan, magenta and yellow) and 'key' (black) it contains. Black is referred to as K so as not to cause confusion with the B (blue) in the RGB (red, green, blue) colour model.

Dashboard *(web)*: A user interface or webpage that gives an overview of important metrics related to the website or business. Alternatively, a dashboard is also a portal that gives access to key tools on the website.

Distributed accountability: A strategy for managing website content where the content is outsourced to a number of different people (probably subject-matter experts) and those people have ultimate authority to sign off on their specific pieces of content. This allows content to be approved quickly, but can lead to inconsistencies if the different experts don't adhere to the organisation's style guide.

Domain name: An internet address used to identify a specific IP address. The domain name is one part of the overall URL; for example, in http://www.pureartscommunications.com/books, the domain name is pureartscommunications.com.

Domain name registrar: An organisation or commercial entity that manages the reservation of Internet domain names.

DSLR: Digital single-lens reflex camera—a digital camera that, like a single-lens reflex camera (SLR), uses a mirror-and-prism system, but combines this with a digital imaging sensor rather than photographic film. Most modern high-end cameras are DSLRs.

E-work: Where work is done remotely (e.g. from home) via the Internet rather than being present in a physical office. E-workers may be employees working from home or freelancers working as independent contractors.

Earned social media strategy: Brand exposure through public acceptance and a strong emotional connection with your organisation (e.g. word of mouth, exposure by media outlets, or endorsement by influencers).

Embed *(web)***:** On a webpage, an embedded file is any type of multimedia file that is inserted directly into the page (rather than viewed through a third-party plugin).

Engagement: When your followers engage with something you've posted by liking, sharing or commenting on it. Different social networks have different ways of engaging, but they all tend to be built around these three main approaches.

File sharing: The practice of making computer files available to other users of a network. File sharing may be legal or illegal, depending on the type of material being shared (e.g. a document shared with collaborators through a cloud storage service; piracy of music or videos via the Internet).

Findability: The ease with which information on a website can be found, both from outside the website (e.g. using search engines) and by users already on the website.

Follower/fan: A person who has chosen to follow you on social media so that your posts appear automatically in their news feed.

Geotag: An electronic tag that assigns a geographical location to a photograph, video, social media post etc.

Hashtag: A way of categorising topics on social media, especially Twitter and Instagram. A hashtag is a group of words prefaced by the # symbol. Users can search for a specific hashtag and read all posts that use that tag.

HTML5: The most recent iteration of the Hypertext Markup Language (HTML), the standard programming language for describing the contents and appearance of webpages.

Inclusive language: Language that avoids the use of expressions, phrases or words that may be seen to exclude or discriminate against particular groups (e.g. 'mankind').

Information architecture: The structure of a website, also known as navigation—the menus and internal links used to find things on a site.

Interaction design: Where things are located on a webpage—the placement of content like videos or paragraphs of text.

Internet: The global system of interconnected computer networks that use the Internet protocol suite (TCP/IP) to link devices worldwide. As well as carrying the linked hypertext documents of the World Wide Web (i.e. websites), the Internet also has other uses such as email, telephony and peer-to-peer file-sharing.

iOS: The mobile operating system that powers all Apple mobile devices—iPhone, iPad, iPod and Apple Watch. Its major competitor is Google's Android operating system.

IP (internet protocol) address: A unique string of numbers separated by full stops that identifies each computer using the Internet Protocol to communicate over a network.

Keywords: Words that users put into search engines when they're looking for a website.

Listicle: A portmanteau of 'list' and 'article'—an online article that gives the reader information in the form of a list (e.g. 'Seven ways to improve your search engine optimisation').

Mention: Social media usernames prefaced by the @ symbol, used to reply to or identify specific people, especially on Twitter and Instagram.

Metadata: An underlying definition or description—data that gives information about other data.

Monetise: To add components to a website that make the owner money, such as advertising or an online store.

Navigation *(web)*: How a user finds content on a website. Some examples of navigation are menus, links and internal search engines.

Op-ed: Opinion piece in a newspaper (short for 'opposite the editorial').

Original content: Something shared on social media that you've created yourself, such as a blog post or photos.

Owned social media strategy: Branded properties that you control and can use strategically, such as your website, blog or social channels. A content strategy would be an owned strategy (e.g. producing content for your blog then publicising it on your social channels). Word-of-mouth exposure through your members is also an owned strategy—you can empower your members so that they want to talk about your organisation naturally in their own online channels.

Pageview: An instance of an internet user visiting a specific page on a website.

Paid social media strategy: A social advertising strategy (such as boosted Facebook posts or promoted tweets). This involves boosting certain posts that were already popular with your audience, hopefully resulting in a boost to your earned strategy in the form of likes and shares, or developing standalone ads.

Pay-per-click (PPC): A form of online advertising where you pay a certain amount for every click the ad generates to your nominated website.

Plugin: A software component that adds a specific feature to an existing computer program.

Podcast: A portmanteau of 'iPod' and 'broadcast'— a digital audio file, usually part of a themed series, that can be downloaded from a website to a media player (such as a mobile device) or computer. Subscribers receive updates automatically.

Raster image: An image format made up of pixels—thousands of little squares that collectively create an image. Photos are raster images. Raster images can only be blown up to a certain size before they start to lose definition and become pixelated.

Reach: The number of people who see the things you post on your social media account. This is usually divided into *organic reach* and *paid reach*. Organic reach is the number of people who see your posts without you having to pay to 'boost' or advertise them. Paid reach is the number of people you reach with an advertisement or boosted post.

Repurposing: Using content across more than one medium (e.g. website and social media).

Responsive: A website that adapts itself when it's viewed on devices such as smartphones or tablets, usually changing some aspects of the layout, including the menus.

Rich media: Specific installations on the web that are more functional and interactive (i.e. not just text or static images). These include video, interactive images (such as those that change when a mouse rolls over them) or interactive graphics. Usually used in the context of marketing and advertising.

RGB: An additive colour model in which red, green and blue are mixed together to produce a broad array of colours. The RGB model is used in electronic devices such as televisions, digital cameras, computer monitors, image scanners, etc.; however, different devices will detect or reproduce RGB values differently, so the actual colour may vary between devices.

Colours can be expressed in a numerical triplet (e.g. 132, 202, 161) that indicates how much of each colour is present (from 0 to 255). If all components are at 0 the result is black; if all are at 255 the result is white.

Scannability: The ease with which a particular piece of text can be read (or scanned) and understood by the target reader. Usually used in the context of online marketing and advertising—good scannability will increase the reader's engagement with the content.

Screen reader: A software application that allows visually impaired people to use a computer by converting text into synthesised speech or feeding it to a Braille output device.

Search engine: A program that allows users to find content on particular websites by entering a keyword, phrase or subject.

Search engine optimisation (SEO): a collection of methods and techniques that aims to increase the number of visitors to a website by ensuring that the website appears high on the list of results returned by a search engine.

Sentiment: How people feel about your brand, as evidenced in the tone of the comments they leave on your social media pages. Sentiment is usually more important than the number of comments.

Self-hosting: Having your website totally under your control, rather than using a platform such as Wix or Squarespace.

Serif: A slight projection finishing off a stroke of a letter in certain typefaces. Typefaces that don't use serifs are known as 'sans serif'. Serif fonts are considered easier to read than sans serif fonts in print, while sans serif fonts are typically used more than serif fonts in content designed to be read on screens.

Server: A computer, device or program dedicated to managing network resources.

Slurl: Domain names that unintentionally have a double meaning, often crude or sexual, arising from when combinations of words can be viewed in several ways. The term is a portmanteau of 'slur' and 'URL'.

Social media coordinator: Publishes content, monitors engagement and responds to comments and questions.

Social media director: Responsible for higher-level planning and final approval of the social media budget, campaigns and strategies.

Social media manager: Oversees the day-to-day running of campaigns and will manage the timelines to ensure that campaign elements are released on time.

Social media management tool: An online program that allows you to see all your social media channels in one dashboard and post to them from the one place, rather than having to log in to them separately. Social media management tools also let you schedule posts and often have quite in-depth analytics.

Structural/semantic mark-up: In web design, applying HTML tags to indicate the content's intended meaning or purpose (e.g. <h1> indicates a major heading, <h2> indicates a sub-heading, and <h3> indicates a minor heading) rather than for stylistic reasons.

Style guide (visual): A document that sets out all the elements related to a brand's appearance, presentation and design. This helps ensure consistency across all publicity material, whether physical or online, and between designers.

Style guide (written): A document that contains details of the way an organisation expects its content to be written.

Traditional media: Newspapers, radio and television, as opposed to 'new' (online) media. This distinction is becoming increasingly blurred, however, as many traditional news organisations now have a significant online presence, and many 'new' media outlets now have similar credibility to their traditional cousins.

Troll: (Verb) to post inflammatory or inappropriate messages or comments online for the purpose of upsetting other users and provoking a response; (noun) a person who engages in the act of trolling.

URL: Uniform Resource Locator—the global address of documents and other resources on the World Wide Web. The first part of a URL, the protocol identifier, indicates which protocol to use (e.g. http or https), while the second part, the resource indicator, specifies the IP address or domain name where the resource can be found. Specific file names appear after the domain name (e.g. http://www.pureartscommunications.com/books.html tells the browser to fetch the 'Books' webpage—an HTML file—from the pureartscommunications.com domain, using the HTTP protocol).

Vector image: An image format made up of 'paths', which each have a 'vector' (a mathematical formula) that tells the path how it's shaped and the colours it's bordered by. Line illustrations such as cartoons are usually vector images. Vector images can be scaled to any size without losing fidelity.

Web host: A company that provides server space and other services for websites owned by clients who do not have their own servers.

World Wide Web: An information system on the Internet that allows documents to be connected to other documents by hypertext links, enabling the user to search for information by moving from one document to another. Note: The Internet is the physical network infrastructure; the World Wide Web is the system of documents (e.g. websites) overlayed on it. The Web is the primary tool most people use to access the Internet, but not all Internet servers are part of the World Wide Web.

Further Reading

Copyright and intellectual property

APRA AMCOS (Australia, NZ and Pacific) — http://apraamcos.com.au

Copyright Agency (Australia, NZ and Pacific) — http://copyright.com.au

Creative Commons — http://creativecommons.org.au

Graphic design

Adobe Creative Suite 6 video tutorials — https://helpx.adobe.com/creative-suite.html

Canva Design School — https://designschool.canva.com/

Lupton, Ellen and Cole Phillips, Jennifer, *Graphic Design: The New Basics*, Princeton Architectural Press, second edition 2015.

Photography and videography

About Tech, *Photography* — http://photography.about.com/

Fenchel & Janisch, 'The Ultimate Introduction to DSLR Filmmaking—Basic Tutorial', *YouTube*, https://www.youtube.com/watch?v=w8BzeZEGEYY

iPhone Photography School — http://iphonephotographyschool.com/

Photography Concentrate, *Smartphone Photography 101* — http://photographyconcentrate.com/introduction-to-smartphone-photography/

Shaw, David, 'The Five Most Essential Camera Settings and How to Use Them', *Digital Photography School* — http://digital-photography-school.com/essential-camera-settings/

Vimeo Video School, *Video 101* — https://vimeo.com/blog/post/video-101-choosing-a-camera

Event promotion

Pinkham, Ryan, '50 Helpful Resources for Planning, Promoting, and Running a Successful Event', *Constant Contact* — https://blogs.constantcontact.com/resources-planning-events/

University of Illinois, *Marketing and Advertising Handbook* — http://publicaffairs.illinois.edu/eventplanning/Marketing%20and%20Advertising%20Handbook.pdf

Web design

Australian Domain Name Administrator — https://www.auda.org.au/

Microsoft Office Support, *Accessibility Checker* — https://support.office.com/en-us/article/Use-the-Accessibility-Checker-on-your-Windows-desktop-to-find-accessibility-issues-a16f6de0-2f39-4a2b-8bd8-5ad801426c7f?ui=en-US&rs=en-US&ad=US

Moz, *The Beginner's Guide to Content Marketing* — https://moz.com/beginners-guide-to-content-marketing

Moz, *The Beginner's Guide to SEO*—https://moz.com/beginners-guide-to-seo

Nielsen, Jakob, *F-shaped Pattern for Reading Web Content*—https://www.nngroup.com/articles/f-shaped-pattern-reading-web-content/

Nielsen, Jakob, *How Users Read on the Web*—http://www.nngroup.com/articles/how-users-read-on-the-web/

Samson, Melinda, 'Beyond Google Search: 3 Other Places Your AdWords Ads Can Appear', *Click-Winning Content* — http://clickwinningcontent.com.au/adwords-take-your-business/

US Department of Health and Human Services, *Usability Portal* — https://www.usability.gov/

UX Movement, *6 Surprising Bad Practices That Hurt Dyslexic Users* — http://uxmovement.com/content/6-surprising-bad-practices-that-hurt-dyslexic-users/

WAVE, *Web Accessibility Evaluation Tool* — http://wave.webaim.org/

Wikipedia, *List of Web Analytics Software* — https://en.wikipedia.org/wiki/List_of_web_analytics_software

World Wide Web Consortium, *Accessibility* — http://www.w3.org/standards/webdesign/accessibility

Social media

Adespresso, *Lead Generation with Facebook Ads: The Definitive Guide* — https://adespresso.com/academy/blog/lead-generation-facebook-ads-definitive-guide/

Business News Daily, *Tumblr for Business: Everything You Need to Know* — http://www.businessnewsdaily.com/7455-tumblr-for-business.html

Facebook, *Facebook Business* — https://www.facebook.com/business/

Small Business Trends, *What is Periscope and How Do I Use It?* — https://smallbiztrends.com/2015/08/what-is-periscope-how-do-i-use-it.html

Zephoria, *The Top 20 Valuable Facebook Statistics* — https://zephoria.com/top-15-valuable-facebook-statistics/

Media writing and interview skills

Kuehn, Scott A. and Lingwall, Andrew, *The Basics of Media Writing: A Strategic Approach*, CQ Press, 2017.

Lee, Carolyne, *Power Prose: Writing Skills for the Media Age*, Hardie Grant Books, 2004.

Taylor, Robert, *Media Interview Techniques: A Complete Guide to Media Training*, Kogan Page, 2015.

The Balance, *Media Writing Tips* — https://www.thebalance.com/media-writing-tips-4073716

Writing

Chicago Manual of Style Online — http://www.chicagomanualofstyle.org/home.html

Cutts, Martin, *The Oxford Guide to Plain English*, Oxford University Press, 2013.

Fogarty, Mignon, *Grammar Girl* — http://www.quickanddirtytips.com/grammar-girl

Institute of Professional Editors, *About Editing* — http://iped-editors.org/About_editing.aspx

Orwell, George, *Politics and the English Language* — https://ebooks.adelaide.edu.au/o/orwell/george/o79p/

Strunk, William and White, E.B., *The Elements of Style*, Pearson, fourth edition 1999.

UK Government, *How People Read* — https://www.gov.uk/guidance/content-design/writing-for-gov-uk#how-people-read

Wikipedia, *Simplified Technical English* — https://en.wikipedia.org/wiki/Simplified_Technical_English

www.ingramcontent.com/pod-product-compliance
Lightning Source LLC
Chambersburg PA
CBHW040929030426
42334CB00002B/9